PENGUIN CLASSICS

TWELFTH NIGHT

T. J. B. SPENCER, sometime Director of the Shakespeare Institute of the University of Birmingham, was the founding editor of the New Penguin Shakespeare, for which he edited both *Romeo and Juliet* and *Hamlet*.

STANLEY WELLS is Honorary President of the Shakespeare Birthplace Trust, Emeritus Professor of Shakespeare Studies at the University of Birmingham, and General Editor of the Oxford Shakespeare. His many books include *Shakespeare: For All Time*, *Shakespeare & Co.*, *Shakespeare, Sex, and Love* and *Great Shakespeare Actors*.

M. M. MAHOOD is an Emeritus Professor of English Literature at the University of Kent. She is the author of *Shakespeare's Wordplay* and *Playing Bit Parts in Shakespeare*, and edited *The Merchant of Venice* in the New Cambridge Shakespeare series.

MICHAEL DOBSON is Professor of Shakespeare Studies and Director of the Shakespeare Institute of the University of Birmingham. His publications include *The Making of the National Poet*, *The Oxford Companion to Shakespeare* (with Stanley Wells), *England's Elizabeth: An Afterlife in Fame and Fantasy* (with Nicola Watson), and *Shakespeare and Amateur Performance: A Cultural History*.

WILLIAM SHAKESPEARE

Twelfth Night

Edited with a Commentary by
M. M. MAHOOD
and with an Introduction by
MICHAEL DOBSON

PENGUIN BOOKS

PENGUIN CLASSICS

UK | USA | Canada | Ireland | Australia
India | New Zealand | South Africa

Penguin Books is part of the Penguin Random House group of companies
whose addresses can be found at global.penguinrandomhouse.com.

This edition first published in Penguin Books 1969
Reissued in the Penguin Shakespeare series 2010
Reissued in Penguin Classics 2015

009

This edition copyright © Penguin Books, 1968
Account of the Text and Commentary copyright © M. M. Mahood, 1968
General Introduction and Chronology copyright © Stanley Wells, 2005
Introduction, The Play in Performance and
Further Reading copyright © Michael Dobson, 2005
All rights reserved

The moral rights of the editors have been asserted

Set in Postscript Monotype Fournier
Typeset by Palimpsest Book Production Limited, Falkirk, Stirlingshire
Printed in Great Britain by Clays Ltd, Elcograf S.p.A

ISBN: 978–0–141–39644–6

Contents

General Introduction

Every play by Shakespeare is unique. This is part of his greatness. A restless and indefatigable experimenter, he moved with a rare amalgamation of artistic integrity and dedicated professionalism from one kind of drama to another. Never shackled by convention, he offered his actors the alternation between serious and comic modes from play to play, and often also within the plays themselves, that the repertory system within which he worked demanded, and which provided an invaluable stimulus to his imagination. Introductions to individual works in this series attempt to define their individuality. But there are common factors that underpin Shakespeare's career.

Nothing in his heredity offers clues to the origins of his genius. His upbringing in Stratford-upon-Avon, where he was born in 1564, was unexceptional. His mother, born Mary Arden, came from a prosperous farming family. Her father chose her as his executor over her eight sisters and his four stepchildren when she was only in her late teens, which suggests that she was of more than average practical ability. Her husband John, a glover, apparently unable to write, was nevertheless a capable businessman and loyal townsfellow, who seems to have fallen on relatively hard times in later life. He would have been brought up as a Catholic, and may have retained

Catholic sympathies, but his son subscribed publicly to Anglicanism throughout his life.

The most important formative influence on Shakespeare was his school. As the son of an alderman who became bailiff (or mayor) in 1568, he had the right to attend the town's grammar school. Here he would have received an education grounded in classical rhetoric and oratory, studying authors such as Ovid, Cicero and Quintilian, and would have been required to read, speak, write and even think in Latin from his early years. This classical education permeates Shakespeare's work from the beginning to the end of his career. It is apparent in the self-conscious classicism of plays of the early 1590s such as the tragedy of *Titus Andronicus*, *The Comedy of Errors*, and the narrative poems *Venus and Adonis* (1592–3) and *The Rape of Lucrece* (1593–4), and is still evident in his latest plays, informing the dream visions of *Pericles* and *Cymbeline* and the masque in *The Tempest*, written between 1607 and 1611. It inflects his literary style throughout his career. In his earliest writings the verse, based on the ten-syllabled, five-beat iambic pentameter, is highly patterned. Rhetorical devices deriving from classical literature, such as alliteration and antithesis, extended similes and elaborate wordplay, abound. Often, as in *Love's Labour's Lost* and *A Midsummer Night's Dream*, he uses rhyming patterns associated with lyric poetry, each line self-contained in sense, the prose as well as the verse employing elaborate figures of speech. Writing at a time of linguistic ferment, Shakespeare frequently imports Latinisms into English, coining words such as abstemious, addiction, incarnadine and adjunct. He was also heavily influenced by the eloquent translations of the Bible in both the Bishops' and the Geneva versions. As his experience grows, his verse and prose become more supple,

the patterning less apparent, more ready to accommo-
date the rhythms of ordinary speech, more colloquial in
diction, as in the speeches of the Nurse in *Romeo and
Juliet*, the characterful prose of Falstaff and Hamlet's
soliloquies. The effect is of increasing psychological
realism, reaching its greatest heights in *Hamlet, Othello,
King Lear, Macbeth* and *Antony and Cleopatra*. Gradually
he discovered ways of adapting the regular beat of the
pentameter to make it an infinitely flexible instrument for
matching thought with feeling. Towards the end of his
career, in plays such as *The Winter's Tale, Cymbeline* and
The Tempest, he adopts a more highly mannered style,
in keeping with the more overtly symbolical and emblem-
atical mode in which he is writing.

So far as we know, Shakespeare lived in Stratford till
after his marriage to Anne Hathaway, eight years his
senior, in 1582. They had three children: a daughter,
Susanna, born in 1583 within six months of their marriage,
and twins, Hamnet and Judith, born in 1585. The next
seven years of Shakespeare's life are virtually a blank.
Theories that he may have been, for instance, a schoolmaster, or a lawyer, or a soldier, or a sailor, lack evidence
to support them. The first reference to him in print, in
Robert Greene's pamphlet *Greene's Groatsworth of Wit*
of 1592, parodies a line from *Henry VI, Part III*, implying
that Shakespeare was already an established playwright.
It seems likely that at some unknown point after the birth
of his twins he joined a theatre company and gained
experience as both actor and writer in the provinces and
London. The London theatres closed because of plague
in 1593 and 1594; and during these years, perhaps recognizing the need for an alternative career, he wrote and
published the narrative poems *Venus and Adonis* and *The
Rape of Lucrece*. These are the only works we can be

certain that Shakespeare himself was responsible for putting into print. Each bears the author's dedication to Henry Wriothesley, Earl of Southampton (1573–1624), the second in warmer terms than the first. Southampton, younger than Shakespeare by ten years, is the only person to whom he personally dedicated works. The Earl may have been a close friend, perhaps even the beautiful and adored young man whom Shakespeare celebrates in his *Sonnets*.

The resumption of playing after the plague years saw the founding of the Lord Chamberlain's Men, a company to which Shakespeare was to belong for the rest of his career, as actor, shareholder and playwright. No other dramatist of the period had so stable a relationship with a single company. Shakespeare knew the actors for whom he was writing and the conditions in which they performed. The permanent company was made up of around twelve to fourteen players, but one actor often played more than one role in a play and additional actors were hired as needed. Led by the tragedian Richard Burbage (1568–1619) and, initially, the comic actor Will Kemp (d. 1603), they rapidly achieved a high reputation, and when King James I succeeded Queen Elizabeth I in 1603 they were renamed as the King's Men. All the women's parts were played by boys; there is no evidence that any female role was ever played by a male actor over the age of about eighteen. Shakespeare had enough confidence in his boys to write for them long and demanding roles such as Rosalind (who, like other heroines of the romantic comedies, is disguised as a boy for much of the action) in *As You Like It*, Lady Macbeth and Cleopatra. But there are far more fathers than mothers, sons than daughters, in his plays, few if any of which require more than the company's normal complement of three or four boys.

The company played primarily in London's public playhouses – there were almost none that we know of in the rest of the country – initially in the Theatre, built in Shoreditch in 1576, and from 1599 in the Globe, on Bankside. These were wooden, more or less circular structures, open to the air, with a thrust stage surmounted by a canopy and jutting into the area where spectators who paid one penny stood, and surrounded by galleries where it was possible to be seated on payment of an additional penny. Though properties such as cauldrons, stocks, artificial trees or beds could indicate locality, there was no representational scenery. Sound effects such as flourishes of trumpets, music both martial and amorous, and accompaniments to songs were provided by the company's musicians. Actors entered through doors in the back wall of the stage. Above it was a balconied area that could represent the walls of a town (as in *King John*), or a castle (as in *Richard II*), and indeed a balcony (as in *Romeo and Juliet*). In 1609 the company also acquired the use of the Blackfriars, a smaller, indoor theatre to which admission was more expensive, and which permitted the use of more spectacular stage effects such as the descent of Jupiter on an eagle in *Cymbeline* and of goddesses in *The Tempest*. And they would frequently perform before the court in royal residences and, on their regular tours into the provinces, in non-theatrical spaces such as inns, guildhalls and the great halls of country houses.

Early in his career Shakespeare may have worked in collaboration, perhaps with Thomas Nashe (1567–c. 1601) in *Henry VI, Part I* and with George Peele (1556–96) in *Titus Andronicus*. And towards the end he collaborated with George Wilkins (*fl.* 1604–8) in *Pericles*, and with his younger colleagues Thomas Middleton (1580–1627), in *Timon of Athens*, and John Fletcher (1579–1625), in *Henry*

VIII, *The Two Noble Kinsmen* and the lost play *Cardenio*. Shakespeare's output dwindled in his last years, and he died in 1616 in Stratford, where he owned a fine house, New Place, and much land. His only son had died at the age of eleven, in 1596, and his last descendant died in 1670. New Place was destroyed in the eighteenth century but the other Stratford houses associated with his life are maintained and displayed to the public by the Shakespeare Birthplace Trust.

One of the most remarkable features of Shakespeare's plays is their intellectual and emotional scope. They span a great range from the lightest of comedies, such as *The Two Gentlemen of Verona* and *The Comedy of Errors*, to the profoundest of tragedies, such as *King Lear* and *Macbeth*. He maintained an output of around two plays a year, ringing the changes between comic and serious. All his comedies have serious elements: Shylock, in *The Merchant of Venice*, almost reaches tragic dimensions, and *Measure for Measure* is profoundly serious in its examination of moral problems. Equally, none of his tragedies is without humour: Hamlet is as witty as any of his comic heroes, *Macbeth* has its Porter, and *King Lear* its Fool. His greatest comic character, Falstaff, inhabits the history plays and *Henry V* ends with a marriage, while *Henry VI, Part III*, *Richard II* and *Richard III* culminate in the tragic deaths of their protagonists.

Although in performance Shakespeare's characters can give the impression of a superabundant reality, he is not a naturalistic dramatist. None of his plays is explicitly set in his own time. The action of few of them (except for the English histories) is set even partly in England (exceptions are *The Merry Wives of Windsor* and the Induction to *The Taming of the Shrew*). Italy is his favoured location. Most of his principal story-lines derive from printed writings; but the structuring and translation of these narratives into dramatic terms is Shakespeare's own, and he invents much additional material. Most of the plays contain elements of myth and legend, and many derive from ancient or more recent history or from romantic tales of ancient times and faraway places. All reflect his reading, often in close detail. Holinshed's *Chronicles* (1577, revised 1587), a great compendium of English, Scottish and Irish history, provided material for his English history plays. The *Lives of the Noble Grecians and Romans* by the Greek writer Plutarch, finely translated into English from the French by Sir Thomas North in 1579, provided much of the narrative material, and also a mass of verbal detail, for his plays about Roman history. Some plays are closely based on shorter individual works: *As You Like It*, for instance, on the novel *Rosalynde* (1590) by his near-contemporary Thomas Lodge (1558–1625), *The Winter's Tale* on *Pandosto* (1588) by his old rival Robert Greene (1558–92) and *Othello* on a story by the Italian Giraldi Cinthio (1504–73). And the language of his plays is permeated by the Bible, the Book of Common Prayer and the proverbial sayings of his day.

Shakespeare was popular with his contemporaries, but his commitment to the theatre and to the plays in performance is demonstrated by the fact that only about half of his plays appeared in print in his lifetime, in slim paperback volumes known as quartos, so called because they were made from printers' sheets folded twice to form four leaves (eight pages). None of them shows any sign that he was involved in their publication. For him, performance was the primary means of publication. The most frequently reprinted of his works were the non-dramatic poems – the erotic *Venus and Adonis* and the more moralistic *The Rape of Lucrece*. The *Sonnets*, which appeared in 1609, under his name but possibly without his consent, were less successful, perhaps because the vogue for sonnet sequences, which peaked in the 1590s, had passed by then. They were not reprinted until 1640, and then only in garbled form along with poems by other writers. Happily, in 1623, seven years after he died, his colleagues John Heminges (1556–1630) and Henry Condell (d. 1627) published his collected plays, including eighteen that had not previously appeared in print, in the first Folio, whose name derives from the fact that the printers' sheets were folded only once to produce two leaves (four pages). Some of the quarto editions are badly printed, and the fact that some plays exist in two, or even three, early versions creates problems for editors. These are discussed in the Account of the Text in each volume of this series.

Shakespeare's plays continued in the repertoire until the Puritans closed the theatres in 1642. When performances resumed after the Restoration of the monarchy in 1660 many of the plays were not to the taste of the times, especially because their mingling of genres and failure to meet the requirements of poetic justice offended against the dictates of neoclassicism. Some, such as *The Tempest* (changed by John Dryden and William Davenant in 1667 to suit contemporary taste), *King Lear* (to which Nahum Tate gave a happy ending in 1681) and *Richard III* (heavily adapted by Colley Cibber in 1700 as a vehicle for his own talents), were extensively rewritten; others fell into neglect. Slowly they regained their place in the repertoire, and they continued to be reprinted, but it was not until the great actor David Garrick (1717–79) organized a spectacular jubilee in Stratford in 1769 that Shakespeare began to be regarded as a transcendental

genius. Garrick's idolatry prefigured the enthusiasm of
critics such as Samuel Taylor Coleridge (1772–1834) and
William Hazlitt (1778–1830). Gradually Shakespeare's
reputation spread abroad, to Germany, America, France
and to other European countries.

During the nineteenth century, though the plays were
generally still performed in heavily adapted or abbreviated versions, a large body of scholarship and criticism
began to amass. Partly as a result of a general swing in
education away from the teaching of Greek and Roman
texts and towards literature written in English,
Shakespeare became the object of intensive study in
schools and universities. In the theatre, important turning
points were the work in England of two theatre directors, William Poel (1852–1934) and his disciple Harley
Granville-Barker (1877–1946), who showed that the
application of knowledge, some of it newly acquired, of
early staging conditions to performance of the plays could
render the original texts viable in terms of the modern
theatre. During the twentieth century appreciation of
Shakespeare's work, encouraged by the availability of
audio, film and video versions of the plays, spread around
the world to such an extent that he can now be claimed
as a global author.

The influence of Shakespeare's works permeates the
English language. Phrases from his plays and poems –
'a tower of strength', 'green-eyed jealousy', 'a foregone
conclusion' – are on the lips of people who may never
have read him. They have inspired composers of songs,
orchestral music and operas; painters and sculptors; poets,
novelists and film-makers. Allusions to him appear in pop
songs, in advertisements and in television shows. Some
of his characters – Romeo and Juliet, Falstaff, Shylock
and Hamlet – have acquired mythic status. He is valued

for his humanity, his psychological insight, his wit and
humour, his lyricism, his mastery of language, his ability
to excite, surprise, move and, in the widest sense of the
word, entertain audiences. He is the greatest of poets,
but he is essentially a dramatic poet. Though his plays
have much to offer to readers, they exist fully only in
performance. In these volumes we offer individual introductions, notes on language and on specific points of the
text, suggestions for further reading and information
about how each work has been edited. In addition we
include accounts of the ways in which successive gener-
ations of interpreters and audiences have responded to
challenges and rewards offered by the plays. The Penguin
Shakespeare series aspires to remove obstacles to understanding and to make pleasurable the reading of the work
of the man who has done more than most to make us
understand what it is to be human.

Stanley Wells

The Chronology of
Shakespeare's Works

A few of Shakespeare's writings can be fairly precisely dated. An allusion to the Earl of Essex in the chorus to Act V of *Henry V*, for instance, could only have been written in 1599. But for many of the plays we have only vague information, such as the date of publication, which may have occurred long after composition, the date of a performance, which may not have been the first, or a list in Francis Meres's book *Palladis Tamia*, published in 1598, which tells us only that the plays listed there must have been written by that year. The chronology of the early plays is particularly difficult to establish. Not everyone would agree that the first part of *Henry VI* was written after the third, for instance, or *Romeo and Juliet* before *A Midsummer Night's Dream*. The following table is based on the 'Canon and Chronology' section in *William Shakespeare: A Textual Companion*, by Stanley Wells and Gary Taylor, with John Jowett and William Montgomery (1987), where more detailed information and discussion may be found.

The Two Gentlemen of Verona	1590–91
The Taming of the Shrew	1590–91
Henry VI, Part II	1591
Henry VI, Part III	1591

Henry VI, Part I (perhaps with Thomas Nashe)   1592
Titus Andronicus (perhaps with George Peele)   1592
Richard III   1592–3
Venus and Adonis (poem)   1592–3
The Rape of Lucrece (poem)   1593–4
The Comedy of Errors   1594
Love's Labour's Lost   1594–5
Edward III (authorship uncertain,   not later than 1595
    not included in this series)   (printed in 1596)
Richard II   1595
Romeo and Juliet   1595
A Midsummer Night's Dream   1595
King John   1596
The Merchant of Venice   1596–7
Henry IV, Part I   1596–7
The Merry Wives of Windsor   1597–8
Henry IV, Part II   1597–8
Much Ado About Nothing   1598
Henry V   1598–9
Julius Caesar   1599
As You Like It   1599–1600
Hamlet   1600–1601
Twelfth Night   1600–1601
'The Phoenix and the Turtle' (poem)   by 1601
Troilus and Cressida   1602
The Sonnets (poems)   1593–1603 and later
Measure for Measure   1603
A Lover's Complaint (poem)   1603–4
Sir Thomas More (in part,
    not included in this series)   1603–4
Othello   1603–4
All's Well That Ends Well   1604–5
Timon of Athens (with Thomas Middleton)   1605
King Lear   1605–6

Introduction

'If music be the food of love, play on . . .' The first line of *Twelfth Night* is now so famous, even independently of what has become one of the best-loved comedies ever written, that we are in danger of overlooking what an extraordinary opening gambit for a play it is. An important, aristocratic character arrives on the stage, attended by courtiers (in the theatre, we won't gather until the following scene that his name is Orsino, and he is Duke of Illyria), and at the play's first performances this entrance was probably the cue for the theatre's consort of musicians – who may have been entertaining the waiting audience for as long as an hour beforehand – to cease playing. But instead of getting on with whatever story he will turn out to be in, Orsino would rather join us in listening to yet more of the overture. This first utterance of his, telling the musicians not to stop but to continue, doesn't so much start the play off as postpone it. Beginning with a man putting music before action in the name of love, *Twelfth Night* is perhaps Shakespeare's most lyrical play: it can't be a mere accident that he chose to set it in a country whose name enfolds the word 'lyre', nor that he called its heroine Viola, a name shared not only with a flower but also with a musical instrument (the viola da gamba, mentioned within a few lines of her

first exit, at I.3.23–4). Depicting the complicated fortunes
of twins shipwrecked in a strange land, and recounting
the most devastating practical joke ever played on an
overweening servant, *Twelfth Night* certainly doesn't lack
for plot; but it doesn't lack pensive interludes in that plot
either, often provided in the form of songs. The whole
play works as much like a musical composition as like an
adventure story or a farce, and if Orsino's first line doesn't
immediately start the action, it certainly signals some of
the principal themes on which Shakespeare's comedy will
develop a series of exquisite variations. The words 'if',
'music', 'food' and 'love' resonate throughout *Twelfth
Night*; it is a meditative as well as a very funny and
affecting play, reflecting on the springs and implications
of the comedy in which, by this mid-point in his career,
Shakespeare was already supremely accomplished.
Familiar as it has become, it is as self-consciously experi-
mental a play as Shakespeare ever wrote, expanding the
limits of romantic comedy to incorporate a range of
emotional effects unequalled in English comedy.

Although we only learn that this self-indulgent lover's
territory is called Illyria in the second scene of the play,
we have a vivid sense of its atmosphere from the outset.
This sense of a local atmosphere will matter in *Twelfth
Night* more than in many of Shakespeare's previous
comedies, since the play is comparatively unusual in the
thoroughness with which it confines its characters to this
single realm. It is true that one of Shakespeare's earlier
plays, *The Comedy of Errors* (1594), is set entirely in
Ephesus, during one mad day in which the lives of
Antipholus and his servant Dromio are thrown into hilarious and terrifying confusion by the arrival of their
respective long-lost identical twins, but if anything the

dramatic focus in *The Comedy of Errors* is more on the
twins who arrive from Syracuse in quest of their apparently settled counterparts, and on the Antipholi's long-
suffering father, Egeon, who is searching for all four,
than on Ephesus alone; for these characters there is definitely a world elsewhere, and it matters. Similarly, France
is a real offstage presence in *Love's Labour's Lost* (1594–5),
even if the action of the play is confined to Navarre's
'little academe'; and in *Much Ado About Nothing* (1598),
equally, although the action all takes place around the
Sicilian city of Messina, many of the characters are only
passing through on their way home from fighting in a
civil war. It is more characteristic, though, for Shakespeare's comedies to take two contrasting locations as
settings, and to incorporate the journeys between them
as major parts of the plot – whether from Verona to
Milan in *The Two Gentlemen of Verona* (1590–91) or from
Padua to Petruchio's house and back in *The Taming of
the Shrew* (1590–91), or from Theseus' court to the wood
near Athens and back in *A Midsummer Night's Dream*
(1595), or from Venice to Belmont to Venice and back to
Belmont in *The Merchant of Venice* (1596–7), or from the
ducal court to the Forest of Arden in *As You Like It*
(1599–1600). In *Twelfth Night*, though, we find ourselves
in Illyria at the outset, and we stay there; the world beyond
comes to us as nothing more substantial than a succession of rumours, whether of the naval engagement in
which the sailor Antonio once fought against Orsino's
fleet on behalf of a rival city-state which is never named
(III.3.25–38) or of the origins of the twins Viola and
Sebastian, children, as Sebastian belatedly tells Antonio,
to 'that Sebastian of Messaline whom I know you have
heard of' (II.1.15–16). Beyond the fact that he had a mole
upon his brow and died on their thirteenth birthday

(V.1.239–42), we ourselves hear nothing else whatsoever of Sebastian senior, and still less of Messaline, a place name which may or may not be a variant on 'Massilia', the Roman name for what is now Marseilles. We never learn where Viola and Sebastian were sailing from when they got shipwrecked in Illyria, nor why, nor where they were going. What the action of the play appears to guarantee, however, eventually pairing them with Illyria's two leading nobles, is that they will never get there. It is appropriate both to Illyria's seductive charm and to its faintly uneasy aura of stasis that when Viola first hears its name at the opening of the second scene – a matter of seconds after Orsino has taken himself off to 'sweet beds of flowers' until further notice – she is immediately, punningly, reminded of the afterlife, playing on its classical name: 'And what should I do in Illyria? | My brother, he is in Elysium' (I.2.3–4). As it will transpire, both twins are actually in Illyria; but, for better and for worse, getting washed up in Illyria may turn out to be rather like dying and going to heaven for both of them.

Where is Illyria? The popularity of *Twelfth Night* in the Anglophone world over the last three centuries, and a widespread sense that this is a festive, light-hearted play in which no one has a real care in the world and all ends happily (a view which the play's text won't necessarily support), has made the word 'Illyria' well-nigh synonymous with 'Arcadia': Illyria, it is usually assumed, is a sunlit never-never land of love and poetry, outside the ordinary historical time in which we mere mortals are trapped, and only coincidentally to be found on any real map, if at all. There is something in this – though, from Orsino's rather willed and short-lived surrender to music onwards, it might be truer to say that the play rather depicts people who would like to feel that they are in such an Illyria. However, it probably did matter to Shakespeare that there really had been a place with the attractive-sounding name of Illyria, and he undoubtedly knew where it was. Illyria was a Roman province along the eastern Adriatic coast opposite Italy; it is mentioned casually, alongside Massilia, as one of the places where a twin has been searching for his brother in the Roman comedy *Menaechmi*, by Plautus. This play had already been used by Shakespeare as a source for *The Comedy of Errors*, and may have suggested the names both of his twins' homeland and of their accidental destination. But Illyria had a darker reputation too: in classical mythology, it was the place where Cadmus, founder of the tragic city of Thebes, had been transformed into a serpent (as Shakespeare would have remembered from his favourite Latin text, Ovid's *Metamorphoses*, IV.559–603), and it was a matter of historical record that ancient Illyria had been infested by pirates (as Shakespeare would have known from his readings in classical histories such as Plutarch's *Lives of the Noble Grecians and Romans*, a book he certainly revisited not long before composing *Twelfth Night*, while working on *Julius Caesar* in 1599). With this reputation in mind, Shakespeare had mentioned Illyria once before, in *Henry VI, Part II* (1591), when the Duke of Suffolk, about to be put to death by the sailors who have captured him in a skirmish of the Wars of the Roses, compares their chief unfavourably with a classical precedent:

Small things make base men proud. This villain here,
Being captain of a pinnace, threatens more
Than Bargulus, the strong Illyrian pirate. (IV.1.106–8)

The word 'Illyria', then, no more connoted a languid

idyll before this play than do the area's present-day names
now – Croatia, Montenegro, Albania. Even the Illyria
depicted in *Twelfth Night*, for all the hothoused courtly
love which suffuses it, is still troubled by piracy. Antonio
warns Sebastian that without a local guide the place may
prove 'Rough and unhospitable' (III.3.11). His own
shadowy past history as a sea-fighter – during which he
took possession of a ship called *The Phoenix* and the
cargo it was bringing home from Crete – marks him out
himself, as far as Orsino is concerned, as a latterday
Bargulus: 'Notable pirate, thou salt-water thief . . .'
(V.1.66). Antonio has risked his life just by accompany-
ing Sebastian into Illyria: it may be a place where almost
everyone we meet is either in love or about to be, but it
is also a place where love can lead to violent death. Given
the name of the ship which the devoted Antonio stands
to die for having captured, it is highly suggestive that at
around the same time as he was writing *Twelfth Night*
Shakespeare was also composing his poem 'The Phoenix
and the Turtle', another work in which the test of truly
selfless love is a willingness to die, here actualized in the
fates of the allegorical phoenix and its beloved turtle-
dove. The choice of Illyria as a setting places love and
escapism alongside danger and death.

If this lethal edge to Illyria's air of amorous reverie
owes something to the Mediterranean past, the play also
affords glimpses of a definitely English present. It is sometimes claimed that all Shakespeare's comedies, despite
their nominal Italian or French or Viennese locations, are
'really' set in Elizabethan England, but this is a simplifi-
cation. It is truer to say that, just as his histories imagine
the past in terms of the present, so Shakespeare's comedies imagine the exotic in terms of the local. Illyria is
both an Adriatic dreamworld and a parallel universe

which shares many features with Shakespeare's England; completely outside mundane historical time but suggestively sharing some of the concerns of 1601, the year of its composition. At once glamorously Italian and locally topical, for instance, Orsino's name may have been borrowed from a real Italian, Don Virginio Orsino, Duke of Bracciano, who visited Elizabeth I's court in 1600–1601 (and before whom Shakespeare's company performed), while among the names of the rest of the cast the Italian and the English are thoroughly intermingled. The countess for whom Orsino sighs has the Italian name of Olivia, while her ill-wishing steward is called Malvolio, clearly a version of the Italian for malevolent, *malevolo* (just as Shakespeare had earlier named Romeo's well-meaning friend Benvolio and his mercurial one Mercutio). Olivia's waiting-gentlewoman, however, mostly called the Italianate 'Maria', is also sometimes the plain English 'Mary' or 'Marian', and her dissolute uncle and his dupe bear the entirely English names of Sir Toby Belch and Sir Andrew Aguecheek. Similarly, though the play isn't obviously a satire designed primarily to comment on the issues of its day – one reason it has so long outlived them – its characters do occasionally drop remarks hinting at pieces of immediate local knowledge shared with their original Elizabethan audiences. 'Then westward ho!' says Viola, attempting to leave Olivia in Act III, scene 1, just the phrase by which boatmen on the nearby Thames would have offered to row wealthier Globe patrons home towards Westminster; some of the songs into which the drunken Sir Toby breaks during the catch scene, Act II, scene 3, had just been published in Robert Jones' *First Book of Airs* (1600); the fool Feste, observing that the word 'element' is 'overworn' (III.1.57), is alluding to a running joke in another play Shakespeare's company

performed in 1601, Thomas Dekker's *Satiromastix*; and
when Maria compares Malvolio's unwontedly creased,
smiling face to 'the new map with the augmentation of
the Indies' (III.2.74–6) she is probably thinking of one
first printed in 1599, in the second edition of Richard
Hakluyt's *Principal Navigations, Voyages and Discoveries
of the English Nation*. Illyria is thus a faraway, once-upon-
a-time place that is also here and now, perhaps most
strikingly when Sebastian and Antonio, arriving in the
danger-fraught city, agree to meet at an inn: 'In the south
suburbs, at the Elephant, | Is best to lodge' (III.3.40–41),
advises Antonio. Suddenly the city of the play is also the
London of its audience. In Shakespeare's day an estab-
lishment called the Elephant did indeed stand in the south
suburbs, in Southwark, serving a clientele which must
have included spectators on their way to and from the
nearby Globe Theatre. In 1601 the effect of Antonio's
casually knowing reference to this familiar building must
have been rather as if two characters in a present-day
film had suddenly gestured out of the screen towards the
foyer and agreed a rendezvous at the cinema's café, just
as Orsino's opening demand for the musicians to play on
would be rather like a film starting with its main character demanding an encore of the theme we have just
heard being played over the opening credits.

In such ways the fragile, fantastical nature of Illyria
is carefully pointed out to us at intervals throughout the
play, and we are allowed to feel that the nominal time of
its action is really coterminous with the present tense of
performance. (When we hear in the last scene that three
months have passed since the shipwreck, we are liable to
feel that Illyria must be akin to those fairy-tale realms
into which mortals are seduced for an afternoon which,
on their return home, turns out to have lasted for years.)

Characters in *Twelfth Night* can occasionally half slip out of Illyria into our reality and pass comment, as they do on the aphrodisiac potential of the incidental music or on the quality of a local inn. Similarly a few of them (principally Viola and Olivia) will confide in us in soliloquy about what they are making of the story, or rather, as it turns out, about what the story is making of them. As is usually the case in Shakespeare's drama, the characters are at once there in the world of the play and here with us in the theatre, and this sense that the dramatis personae are themselves collaborating in the act of dramatic make-believe, through which we are helping to animate them, is intensified in *Twelfth Night* by the way in which they, too, are busily cherishing a series of fanciful hypotheses. It is entirely characteristic that this play should begin with the word 'If', showing Orsino indulging and acting upon the notion that music may be the food of love without actually committing himself as to whether it is or not. It is almost as if the whole of *Twelfth Night* takes place within such a conditional clause – supposing there were an Illyria like this, what if . . . ? One of the main speculations entertained by the play appears to be 'what if there were a country in which everyone spent their time both nurturing their desires and disowning responsibility for them?'

This distinctively Illyrian state of mind is one which the play's chief protagonist Viola appears to fall into within minutes of being brought ashore by the helpful Captain in Act I, scene 2. Suspended in uncertainty as to whether her brother has survived the wreck or not – longing that she 'might not be delivered to the world – | Till I had made my own occasion mellow – | What my estate is' (I.2.43–5) – she at first speculates about going into seclusion with Olivia, who the Captain reports is

herself in mourning for a dead brother, but when she
gathers that this is impossible Viola decides to withdraw
from the world in another way. Effectively, Viola, adopting
a strategy by which she may join Orsino's household
instead without disclosing either her sex or her currently
uncertain social and familial status, suspends her identity
for the entire remainder of the play: she will disappear as
herself ('Conceal me what I am', she urges the Captain),
and reappear only in a conditional identity, masquerading
as a page boy under the name of 'Cesario'. Even we in
the audience won't hear her real name until the last
scene, when she is finally reunited with Sebastian, and we
will never again see her in her own clothes. Almost everything Viola says to anyone else in Illyria is, as a result,
heard by us as if it is spoken in inverted commas. Her
every action is similarly reduced, for her, to a kind of
speculation: 'how would Cesario behave in this situation?
and how far can I risk letting the mask slip in order to
influence events on my own behalf?' Some of her most
important and memorable utterances in the play develop
further hypotheses and conditional clauses too. Sent by
Orsino to woo Olivia on his behalf, for example, Viola
inadvertently captivates Olivia by elaborating a fantasy
of what Cesario would do if he were as passionately
obsessed with her as Orsino is:

VIOLA
    If I did love you in my master's flame,
    With such a suffering, such a deadly life,
    In your denial I would find no sense;
    I would not understand it.
OLIVIA   Why, what would you?
VIOLA
    Make me a willow cabin at your gate,

And call upon my soul within the house;
Write loyal cantons of contemnèd love
And sing them loud even in the dead of night;
Hallow your name to the reverberate hills
And make the babbling gossip of the air
Cry out 'Olivia!' O, you should not rest
Between the elements of air and earth,
But you should pity me.

OLIVIA   You might do much. (I.5.253–65)

The beauty of this celebrated vision of how a rejected
courtly lover might besiege his mistress in part depends
on our knowledge that it is just that, only a vision. No
one is really proposing to undertake this extravagant and
poetical campaign of harassment, and Viola doesn't even
really intend that her description of it should persuade
Olivia to return Orsino's love, since by now she has
fallen in love with him herself. (Nor does it; instead its
combination of courtly eloquence and yearning, orgasmic
'O' sounds excites Olivia in quite another direction, as
her immediate response suggests.) The pathos of Viola's
situation in the play, which has so endeared her to gener-
ations of performers, audiences and anthologists, is that
she finds herself unable to express her hopeless love for
Orsino except by turning herself into just such another
frail poetic hypothesis or fiction. Dismayed by instructions from Orsino to make a further attempt to woo Olivia
for him, Viola can make only a veiled protest of her own
feelings, first tentatively discussing herself as a purely
notional possibility ('were I a woman . . .'), and then
lamenting her own present situation in the third person
and the past tense, as if the real Viola has already
been lost for ever. She tells the sad little story of the
imaginary sister who is really herself with a delicate

compassion which few listeners or readers of this famous
set piece have failed to share:

VIOLA
   My father had a daughter loved a man –
   As it might be perhaps, were I a woman,
   I should your lordship.
ORSINO   And what's her history?
VIOLA
   A blank, my lord. She never told her love,
   But let concealment, like a worm i'the bud,
   Feed on her damask cheek. She pined in thought,
   And with a green and yellow melancholy,
   She sat like Patience on a monument,
   Smiling at grief. (II.4.106–14)

The one reservation which we might feel about this
much-excerpted passage is that Viola, for all her pain,
almost seems to be enjoying her self-pity, every bit as
passively spellbound by the spectacle of her own
lovesickness as Orsino is by his pose as Olivia's scorned
true lover, and certainly Viola shares with the other lovers
in *Twelfth Night* a fatal tendency to watch her feelings
and her story happening to her without making any very
active attempt to intervene. When she realizes that Olivia
has fallen in love with her in her guise as Cesario, for
example, Viola expresses horror at the confusions that
are developing around her but refuses to take any responsibility for clarifying them ('O time, thou must untangle
this, not I! | It is too hard a knot for me t'untie',
II.2.40–41), just as Olivia has let herself fall for Cesario
in the first place by attributing all responsibility for her
emotions and their outcome to an external, predestining
power: 'Fate, show thy force; ourselves we do not owe. |

What is decreed must be, and be this so' (I.5.300–301). Nor is this habit confined to the higher-ranking characters: Malvolio the steward prefaces his daydream about being loved and married by his employer Olivia with the words "Tis but fortune, all is fortune' (II.5.23), and, once falsely convinced that his aspiring love for her is reciprocated, he cries out 'Jove and my stars be praised!' (II.5.165–6). In Illyria, as in the Venice of *Othello*, love is 'a permission of the will' (*Othello*, I.3.331–2) – a point which *Twelfth Night*'s subtitle, *What You Will*, perhaps underlines. One of the factors that enable us to take such comic and aesthetic pleasure in the miseries and humiliations love brings to this play's principal characters is a slight suspicion that they wouldn't suffer from unrequited love nearly so intensely if they didn't have so much irresponsible leisure in which to allow it to flourish. In this atmosphere of amorous languor, it is fitting that Sir Toby Belch can't tell the word 'lechery' from 'lethargy' (I.5.119–20), though even he eventually finds enough energy to parallel and parody his niece Olivia's involvement with a supposed page by contracting a downwardly mobile marriage to a waiting-gentlewoman.

This indolent and unlimited leisure for love is in part a side effect of Illyria's curious demographics, since it is almost without an older generation. In most romantic comedies of the Renaissance, including most of Shakespeare's, the action of the play is driven by lovers' energetic attempts to evade or overcome obstacles and prohibitions placed in the way of their unions, usually by parents. The classic Shakespearian example would be *A Midsummer Night's Dream*, in which 'the sharp Athenian law' (I.1.162) that prompts Hermia and Lysander to elope through the woods is explicitly that which gives fathers the absolute right to marry off their

daughters as they please, regardless of the daughters'
own preferences. In *The Merchant of Venice*, similarly,
Portia can only marry the suitor who successfully under-
goes a test imposed in her late father's will: 'I may neither
choose who I would nor refuse who I dislike,' she
complains, 'so is the will of a living daughter curbed by
the will of a dead father' (I.2.22–4). Even the comparatively untroubled Rosalind of *As You Like It* gets
banished by her wicked uncle just when she has fallen
in love with Orlando, so it's just as well that he too is
obliged to flee to the Forest of Arden at around the same
time by a tyrannous elder brother. For Shakespeare,
romantic comedy is usually generational, telling the story
of how the young succeed in defeating and supplanting
their elders (just as tragedy, by contrast, habitually tells
stories in which children die as a result of their parents'
quarrels and disasters). *Twelfth Night*, though, is conspic-
uously short of such inconvenient seniors. Although it
boasts, in the person of the priggish Malvolio, a comic
antagonist bitterly opposed to much of the revelry that
comedy traditionally stands for, the play is wholly free
of repressive parents – in fact the only survivor of their
generation, Sir Toby Belch, is more unruly and permis-
sive than his juniors. Orsino, already a duke rather than
a mere heir, doesn't need to ask anyone's permission to
marry, and it is perhaps to be understood as symptom-
atic of a habitual preference for music and bowers over
anything as active as hunting (unsuccessfully offered as
an alternative pastime at I.1.16 by the attendant Curio,
who clearly thinks his master ought to get out more)
that at the start of the play he has been eligibly single
ever since Viola was no older than thirteen ('Orsino . . .',
she repeats to the Captain, 'I have heard my father name
him. | He was a bachelor then', I.2.28–9). Olivia lost

her father and her brother in quick succession a year
before the play begins, so that she is a countess in her
own right and similarly accountable to no one (perfectly
at liberty to pursue a marriageable-looking page should
she feel so inclined); and the twins' father, Sebastian of
Messaline, as we've seen, died when they were thirteen,
presumably at least two or three years before their shipwreck. Viola, it is true, can't be quite sure whether her
twin brother is alive or dead – hence in part her
paralysing ignorance as to her 'estate', whether or not
she is still under Sebastian's nominal authority as male
head of the family – but otherwise the play's juvenile
leads are entirely at their own disposal, as we see when
Sebastian so blithely and unhesitatingly consents to
marry Olivia in Act IV, scene 3. *Twelfth Night* isn't a
play in which love either has to escape the obligations
of family and lineage or prove to be compatible with
them but one in which that standard comic quandary
never arises. In this play romantic love is itself the
problem. *Twelfth Night*'s self-regarding central triangle
of Orsino, Olivia and Viola, however sympathetically
and indulgently dramatized, are caught not in their family
circumstances but in their own and one another's
fantasies, prisoners not of heredity but of desire. This,
too, is indicated as early as the play's first scene, when
Orsino ominously compares himself to Actaeon, the
mythical hunter transformed into a stag by the goddess
of chastity and torn to pieces by his own hunting dogs,
and he moralizes this story, as was conventional in the
Renaissance, as an allegory about the perils of sexual
desire:

O, when mine eyes did see Olivia first,
Methought she purged the air of pestilence.

> That instant was I turned into a hart,
> And my desires, like fell and cruel hounds,
> E'er since pursue me. (I.1.20–24)

This image resonates throughout the play: even the witty
servant Maria will be likened by Sir Toby to a beagle,
and her victim Malvolio, destroyed by the consequences
of his own desire for Olivia, will leave the play at its
very end vowing revenge against the whole 'pack' of his
enemies. Desire is the stuff of romantic comedy, but it
is also, as *Twelfth Night* keeps reminding us, a dangerous
thing in which to be caught.

The Illyrian impasse in which desire detains the play's
lovers, and the unprecedented kind of wry and compas-
sionate sexual comedy which it allows Shakespeare to
develop, are beautifully exemplified early in the third act
by a short passage of stichomythia (where two characters engage in a dialogue made especially pointed by their
exchanging single lines of verse). In this scene Viola, on
her second unwilling errand from Orsino to Olivia, is as
ever unable to speak plainly because of the need to maintain her disguise (or is she also too perversely fascinated
by the situation to bring it to an end?), and she finds
herself incapable of dissuading Olivia from seeing
Cesario in the image of her own desires. Almost every
one of the one-line sentences the two women utter is
composed solely of monosyllables, and in performance
such sentences inevitably sound both slower and more
emphatic than longer, fluent ones full of tripping poly-
syllables. They are also full of conditional clauses, introduced by yet another 'if':

OLIVIA
  I prithee, tell me what thou think'st of me?

VIOLA

That you do think you are not what you are.

OLIVIA

If I think so, I think the same of you.

VIOLA

Then think you right; I am not what I am.

OLIVIA

I would you were as I would have you be.

VIOLA

Would it be better, madam, than I am? (III.1.135–40)

The dramatic situation here – of a woman who has unwittingly fallen in love with another woman – is for an audience at once farcical and mildly titillating, and Shakespeare had explored it once before, in *As You Like It*, where the hard-hearted shepherdess Phoebe is punished for her arrogant coldness towards her faithful and eligible suitor Silvius when she develops a hopeless crush on the disguised Rosalind's male alias, Ganymede. In *As You Like It* the situation is scripted primarily for laughs, and the same dramatic irony works comically in *Twelfth Night* too: since we are in on the secret of Cesario's real identity and sex while Olivia isn't, both Olivia's misguided perseverance and Viola's exasperation are very funny. But here they are also observed with a psychological acuteness and seriousness which makes them sufficiently convincing for our laughter to be, in part, a defence against the painful embarrassment of being privy to the way in which Olivia is exposing herself (and to a woman she will end up stuck with for ever as a sister-in-law at that). What is happening to the overwrought countess is comic but also potentially rather cruel, and this graver undertone is highlighted by Viola's riddling and resonant declaration, 'I am not what I am.' Since the phrase 'I am that I am' is one of the titles by which God identified himself to Moses (in Exodus 3:14), Viola – who has already remarked, 'Disguise, I see thou art a wicked- ness | Wherein the pregnant enemy does much' (II.2.27–8) – seems in this negative version of the term to be identifying her duplicitous self with the Devil. (Indeed Shakespeare would reuse the phrase 'I am not what I am' in *Othello*, where it is spoken by the thor- oughly satanic Iago.) Olivia seems to take this point, too: in their next dialogue together (practically a rerun of this one, as though the perplexedly intimate relationship between the two is in a perpetual limbo) she tells Viola, 'A fiend like thee might bear my soul to hell' (III.4.213). In a play where Olivia's steward will discover that one upshot of falling in love can be imprisonment on suspi- cion of demonic possession, this isn't a remark to be taken lightly. Illyria may be as delightfully full of amorous intrigues and misunderstandings as a shared house full of undergraduates, but to appreciate *Twelfth Night*'s full range of moods and emotional effects we need to recog- nize that it is also a seriously dubious state to be in.

Given its preoccupation with idle young people in love, it isn't surprising that *Twelfth Night* should feature a good deal of recreational music, and, as we've seen, it is Orsino's narcissistic interest in using music to work upon his own sensibility in the first scene that sets the tone for much of what is to come in the main love plot. Viola, as if she has guessed this aspect of his character just from learning that he is in love with Olivia, thinks that it is her ability to sing which will recommend her to a posi- tion at his court when she disguises herself as Cesario (I.2.57–60). In the event, however, the play's principal songs are instead provided by a full-time professional,

Feste, who both satirizes his fellow-characters as the play's jester and ministers obediently to their moods as its musician. The songs Shakespeare puts into his plays often crystallize something of their tones and concerns (think of 'Under the greenwood tree' in *As You Like It*, or 'Full fathom five' in *The Tempest*), and the lyrics performed by Feste in two successive scenes of *Twelfth Night*'s second act are no exception. As well as helping further to identify this play's special ambience, a glance at how these songs work within their respective contexts can also serve to remind us of how much the experience of reading a play differs from that of seeing one performed; while an edition of *Twelfth Night*'s text can tell us what words the actors speak and sing in Act II, scenes 3 and 4, there is as yet no technology conveniently available by which it can either act or sing melodies to us. Indeed the earliest printed edition of the play (in the first Folio of Shakespeare's collected plays, published in 1623, seven years after the playwright's death) does not indicate what these songs' melodies originally were. Although an acquaintance of Shakespeare, the composer Thomas Morley, had published an instrumental arrange-ment of a tune called 'O mistress mine' in 1599 (in his *First Book of Consort Lessons*: see The Songs, below), we cannot be sure that this has any connection with the lyric in the play (since a number of other songs of the time began with the same three words), and the earliest extant setting of 'Come away, come away, death' dates from long after Shakespeare's time. But the words themselves indicate the kinds of music they invite – cues which have been taken up on behalf of theatrical producers by some of the most important composers of the last three centuries, among them Thomas Arne, Johannes Brahms, Ralph Vaughan Williams and Paul McCartney – and these

songs have usually been highlights of any live performance of *Twelfth Night*.

Of the two, 'Come away, come away, death' is perhaps
the most straightforward, and the one which is most
fully exploited to colour the scene in which it is sung,
Act II, scene 4. As at the play's opening, Orsino enters
demanding music, specifically requesting, as he greets
Cesario, 'That old and antique song we heard last night'
(II.4.3). For Orsino, part of the appeal of a piece of
music seems to be the way in which it defies time, since
it provides an experience which can be repeated at will:
this old song will be just the same today as it was
yesterday (unless, that is, Orsino's mood changes as it
did during his first speech in the play, I.1.7–8).
Furthermore, a piece of music makes the passage of time
while one is listening to it (on which it depends, and
which it structures) something to be enjoyed aestheti-
cally rather than just regretted, so that for its duration
time's destructive force seems to be suspended, just as
is the action of the play while we and the characters
listen together to the song. Orsino hears 'Come away,
come away, death' in a spirit of pleasing nostalgia, iden-
tifying it as a survival from a lost golden time when love
was always pure (it 'dallies with the innocence of love |
Like the old age', he tells Cesario, II.4.47–8), and, unusually, Shakespeare indicates that its melody is to be played
throughout the intimate dialogue between Orsino and
Cesario which precedes Feste's actual arrival to sing the
words ('Seek him out, and play the tune the while',
instructs the Duke, 14). The tune thus provides a tenderly
melancholy accompaniment, as well as part of the subject
matter, for Viola's first hints to Orsino (understood by
us if not by her interlocutor) that she is in love, and with
him:

ORSINO
  How dost thou like this tune?
VIOLA
  It gives a very echo to the seat
  Where love is throned.
ORSINO   Thou dost speak masterly.
  My life upon't, young though thou art, thine eye
  Hath stayed upon some favour that it loves.
  Hath it not, boy?
VIOLA   A little, by your favour.
ORSINO
  What kind of woman is't?
VIOLA   Of your complexion.
ORSINO
  She is not worth thee, then. What years, i'faith?
VIOLA
  About your years, my lord. (20–28)

When Orsino finally redirects his attention from telling
Cesario about the song to letting Feste get on with singing
it (Feste's 'Are you ready, sir?' (49) may in performance
betray an amused impatience), the lyrics are much as
we might have expected – the passive-aggressive, self-
dramatizing lament of a lover who goes one better than
Orsino by claiming actually to be dying of his unrequited
passion for 'a fair cruel maid'. Like many of Orsino's own
observations on love, it is in the masochistic mainstream
tradition of Renaissance love poetry which traced its
lineage straight back to Francesco Petrarch (1304–74), the
Italian pioneer of the lovelorn sonnet, imitations of whose
stylistic mannerisms and tropes had become clichés of
English verse over the preceding decades:

> Come away, come away, death,
>   And in sad cypress let me be laid.
> Fie away, fie away, breath!
>   I am slain by a fair cruel maid. (II.4.50–53)

Thanks to the way in which this highly orthodox love song is embedded in the scene between Orsino and Viola, though, the experience of seeing and hearing Feste perform it is far richer than are its lyrics alone. We watch the duke and the supposed page listening with an acute sense of the different personal contexts in which they are doing so: to Orsino, the lyrics provide a model for how he imagines the situation between himself and Olivia (perhaps the actor playing him gazes into the distance with self-conscious wistfulness, offering himself to Cesario as the perfect image of the soulful scorned lover), while to Viola the song offers an image at once of her own despair and of its cause, Orsino's apparently unshakeable determination to go on mooning over Olivia. The song freezes them into a tableau, a picture of two people at once companionably sharing a moving piece of music and utterly separated by what we know it means to each of them, so that we ourselves can listen to the music from both their perspectives at once. The time of its performance passes, and the situation between the two listeners doesn't change, but even if the song doesn't exactly help them, its futility becomes itself part of the beauty it confers on this scene.

'O mistress mine', which Feste performs in Act II, scene 3, has an equally conventional lyric, this time in the *carpe diem* tradition by which a poet urges his beloved to seize the opportunity for love before it is too late:

What's to come is still unsure.
In delay there lies no plenty –
Then come kiss me, sweet and twenty,
    Youth's a stuff will not endure. (II.3.47–50)

The effect of the song in context, though, is anything but simple or conventional. Instead of being sung at dawn by a young lover beneath the window of his twenty-year-old beloved, it is performed late at night at the request of the dissipated Sir Toby Belch and his stooge Sir Andrew Aguecheek, and only by accident at that. Relieved that the arrival of Feste will add some musical stimulus to their rather strained attempts at merrymaking, Sir Toby at first requests 'a catch' (a vigorous round, often a drinking song, in which they will all join), but when Feste offers the choice between 'a love song, or a song of good life' (34), Sir Andrew – mistakenly thinking that 'a song of good life', implying a carousing song, means some sort of moralistic hymn or ballad – backs up Sir Toby in choosing a love song instead. The result is a song which both is and isn't appropriate for its onstage audience. The foolish Sir Andrew, detained by Sir Toby at Olivia's house with false and obviously doomed hopes of marrying her while Toby spends his money, certainly needs to be reminded that 'In delay there lies no plenty', but to tell the ageing Sir Toby that 'Youth's a stuff will not endure' is, at best, supremely tactless. He wanted a rowdy party song in which to forget himself, and what he gets is practically a memento mori, a sobering reminder of impending death. In performance, as a result, this song can provide every bit as plangent an interlude as 'Come away, come away, death'. Two of *Twelfth Night*'s screen incarnations have demonstrated this point very effectively. In Trevor Nunn's 1996 film a middle-aged Maria (Imelda Staunton) is also present for Feste's performance, and she tries to catch Sir Toby's eye while awkwardly joining in with the song, hoping that he will get its message and get on with marrying her before it is too late for both of them. Tim Supple's 2003 television version for Channel 4 does without this minor piece of adaptation, but achieves just as telling an effect simply by allowing the camera to dwell in close-up on the ravaged, dissolute face of Sir Toby Belch (David Troughton) as the song is sung and he visibly contemplates his misspent life. In practice, this pretty lyric provides a characteristically Shakespearian moment in which the play's clowns are allowed their share of genuine regrets too. Even the ridiculous Sir Andrew, after all, achieves his share of pathos in this scene, particularly by his subsequent response to Sir Toby's proud claim that he is adored by Maria: 'I was adored once, too' (II.3.174). It is a moot point whether this line is sadder if we think it suddenly opens up the possibility that Sir Andrew has only dwindled into his current self after a past heartbreak, or if we think that he is just trying to keep up with Sir Toby by making what to him will always be an unfounded boast.

Sir Toby, at least, does manage to cheer himself up with a catch immediately after 'O mistress mine' – he, Feste and Sir Andrew sing 'Hold thy peace', and this slighter if louder piece has rather more drastic consequences for the play's narrative. As if to personify the round's nominal content, the steward arrives, specifically in order to request these knaves to hold their peace:

MALVOLIO My masters, are you mad? Or what are you? Have
    you no wit, manners, nor honesty, but to gabble like tinkers

at this time of night? Do ye make an alehouse of my lady's
house, that ye squeak out your coziers' catches without any
mitigation or remorse of voice? Is there no respect of place,
persons, nor time in you? (II.3.85–91)

Malvolio here speaks as perfect a manifesto against
comedy as was ever composed: the whole point of
comedy is to laugh at place, persons and time alike,
delighting in the overturning or at least the suspension
of all order (except perhaps that of the more festive
branches of art – 'We did keep time, sir, in our catches',
retorts Sir Toby, 92). It is one of Shakespeare's most
distinctive traits as a playwright that when he deals with
ideas he prefers to do so in personified form, and Olivia's
joyless and abstemious steward seems to have been
purposely designed to embody everything which opposes
the genre to which this play otherwise belongs. Malvolio's
scenes thus allow Shakespeare to conduct what becomes
a discussion about the nature and ethics of comedy itself.
His status as a specifically anti-comic figure is signalled
from his first remarks in the play, which reproach Feste
and criticize Olivia for indulging him (I.5.70–84), and
the particular role he is given within Olivia's household
makes him both the inevitable provocation and the help-
less butt of the joke to which he will fall victim. As steward
– with responsibility for managing Olivia's estate,
including all the lower servants, such as Maria – he cannot
possibly afford to forfeit his authority by condoning any
revelry among the staff, from whom he is anyway kept
apart by his superior rank, but he is equally kept apart
from the family who employ him, if only by the chain
of office around his neck which marks him out as a
mere upper servant. Confined to this unloved position
as an under-manager, Malvolio is required by his job to

maintain domestic order but prevented from being able
to enforce it (even on Maria) by his status as Sir Toby's
social inferior ('Art any more than a steward?' sneers the
knight, in what is surely the most snobbish and insensi-
tive remark in the play, '. . . Go, sir, rub your chain with
crumbs', II.3.110–11, 115–16). It is no wonder that
Malvolio takes refuge in a consoling erotic fantasy of
upward mobility, his dream of marrying Olivia. Scenting
this secret aspiration with the predatory acuteness of a
hunting dog (II.3.172), Maria will use it to precipitate a
downfall which, though hilarious to watch, almost
deserves to be called tragic, so intimately does Shakespeare dramatize the feelings of the victim of the joke
as well as those of the perpetrators. When we overhear
Malvolio elaborating his fantasy a couple of scenes later,
for example – as Sir Toby, Sir Andrew and Fabian spy
on him in the garden, waiting for him to find the letter
forged by Maria that will convince him that Olivia indeed
loves him – the insulted steward understandably dwells
less on the imagined union with Olivia that might make
him 'Count Malvolio' than on the 'prerogative of speech'
this match would give him finally to be able to berate Sir
Toby for his drunkenness (II.5.34–80). Perhaps this
daydream's most sharply observed and poignant moment
comes when Malvolio, imagining himself fidgeting with
an assumed aristocratic languor while a large retinue of
his personal servants strong-arm a humbled Toby into
his presence, actually has to remind himself that were he
to marry Olivia he would no longer be burdened with
the humiliating accessory which has hitherto defined his
place in the world:

MALVOLIO Seven of my people, with an obedient start, make
  out for him. I frown the while, and perchance wind up my

watch, or play with my (*fingering his steward's chain of office*)
– some rich jewel. (II.5.57–60)

As this detail suggests, Malvolio, for all his programmatic
role as comic antagonist, is as fully psychologized and
realized as any other character in the play: uniformly
serious himself (it is part of the disproportionate punish-
ment meted out by Maria's practical joke that he is even
tricked into smiling), he is taken very seriously by the
play – seriously enough for him to be well worth laughing
at, even if we are almost crying with him at the same
time. What we watch in the Malvolio sub-plot of *Twelfth
Night* is a man being robbed of his privacy and his dignity
'for the love of mockery' and 'in the name of jesting'
(II.5.18–20), and it is clearly part of Shakespeare's design
that the joke at his expense should be sprung comparatively early in the play and should have ceased to be
funny well before the end of it. Malvolio's appearance
to a bemused Olivia in Act III, scene 4, following the
forged letter's instructions, is of course hysterically
funny: among other things, his costume provides a bril-
liant half-indecent visual gag. The bizarre combination
of sober black steward's robes above the waist but gaudy
yellow stockings below makes him half-cleric, half-satyr:
yellow stockings were the traditional masculine badge of
the young, free and single (a popular song of the time,
in which a husband laments the woes of marriage, was
called 'Give me my yellow hose again'). But by Act IV,
with Malvolio confined in the dark as a lunatic, even Sir
Toby is looking for a way out ('I would we were well
rid of this knavery', IV.2.66–7), and Feste, wearying of
taunting Malvolio in the assumed voice of a priest, finally
agrees to provide him with the writing materials which
will enable him to secure his deliverance in the last scene.

In the world of Shakespeare's plays, where the categories
of comedy and tragedy are no more mutually exclusive
than they are in real life, the most hilarious of comic
tours de force may produce perfectly genuine grief.
Indeed, Malvolio's famous parting line, after the decep-
tion practised on him has finally been revealed – 'I'll be
revenged on the whole pack of you!' (V.1.375) – suggests
that to him the only appropriate sequel to the piece of
comedy to which he has been subjected would be a
revenge tragedy. The steward and his sufferings seem
designed to provoke reflections both upon the nature of
comedy and on its potential costs.

In the context of 1601, they provoke reflections, too,
on the religious politics of mirth, since Malvolio's antag-
onism towards Feste is presented as part and parcel of a
more general resistance to festivity and festivals in
general. When Maria is plotting his downfall after his
furious departure from the catch scene, she reports that
'sometimes he is a kind of puritan' (II.3.134), and although
she soon qualifies this remark to suggest that Malvolio's
Puritanism is merely a time-serving affectation (140–45),
it is striking that Shakespeare, who is otherwise so
cautious about referring directly to the religious and political controversies of post-Reformation England, should
use the term 'puritan' at all. Puritanism was a broad movement that wished to steer the Church of England away
from an acceptance that outward conformity with its rites
was the most that could be hoped for and towards an
altogether more zealous and fundamentalist strain of
Christianity; its adherents hoped above all to purge the
English Church of such Catholic practices and celebra-
tions as it still retained. Such ecclesiastical reformers
were definitely on Shakespeare's mind as he wrote *Twelfth
Night*: later in the play he even has Sir Andrew refer

disapprovingly and topically to the Brownists (III.2.30), the followers of the rebel Cambridge theologian Robert Browne, who had set up a separate, independent church of their own in Norwich before being driven into exile in Holland in 1581. Sir Toby, resisting Malvolio's attempts to assert his authority in Act II, scene 3, certainly wants to see himself as the defender of a traditional way of life against a radical upstart. In the same breath with which he scorns Malvolio's social station, Toby deliberately champions the food and drink consumed at the fund-raising parish booze-ups known as 'church-ales' which Puritans were especially keen to abolish: 'Dost thou think, because thou art virtuous, there shall be no more cakes and ale?' (II.3.111–12). Feste follows up this pointed gibe by immediately invoking a saint considerably more popular with Anglo-Catholics than with Puritans, namely the mother of the Blessed Virgin: 'Yes, by Saint Anne, and ginger shall be hot i'the mouth, too' (113–14), and he will later cross-examine the supposed madman for heresy. It is hard to think of *Twelfth Night* as wholly on the side of Sir Toby, who could scarcely be described as one of the High Anglican squirearchy's more shining exemplars, and in practice his defence of cakes and ale may look less like the rallying-cry of a passionate defender of the status quo than another expression of the gluttony that elsewhere, after an over-indulgence in pickled herrings, produces the symptom that gives him his surname (I.5.115–16). But there is no doubt that the play here registers the first stirrings of a contemporary controversy about which forms of recreation were to be deemed morally acceptable, a dispute which would surface more visibly a decade later, when James I would feel compelled to publish a 'Book of Sports' in defence of the various traditional country pursuits which Puritans were actively trying to eradicate (certainly from Sundays, and ideally from the whole week).

Part of that controversy concerned the proper ways in which to celebrate religious holidays, and one of those, of course, gives this play its very title, Twelfth Night. Given the Puritans' widespread objections to the theatre in general, Malvolio's position as a puritanical character in a comedy is hopeless from the outset (appropriately, in the letter scene he is himself placed unwittingly in front of an onstage audience), but it is even more so given that this particular comedy is named after a holiday traditionally associated with just the sorts of disguising, feasting and revelry which Puritans wished to divorce from the Church calendar. The term 'Twelfth Night' is in fact ambiguous – nowadays it is often conflated or confused with Epiphany, the official celebration of the coming of the Magi (6 January), though the actual twelfth day of Christmas is 5 January – but in Shakespeare's time both might provide the occasion for a party. Sir Toby may have such feasts in mind when he sings 'O' the twelfth day of December' (II.3.83), possibly misquoting the still-popular carol 'The Twelve Days of Christmas', and his 'cakes and ale', as well as recalling church-ales, suggest the 'Twelfth Night Cake', a sweet cake with a bean baked in it which would be divided among guests at Twelfth Night parties in order to choose a 'bean king'. The guest who found the bean in his piece of cake would serve as 'Lord of Misrule', a foolish mock-king administering forfeits and healths for the remainder of the occasion. This custom still survives in France, where, incidentally, because the feast of Epiphany goes under a different common name, Shakespeare's play is translated not as *Douxième Nuit* but as *La nuit des rois*. This isn't to say, however, that *Twelfth Night* must have been originally composed for performance on 6 January (though some have tried to argue this), nor that it is set in early January, nor that it is to be understood as entirely preoccupied with the meanings of Christmas parties. (In the theatre, tellingly, attempts to tie the play too closely to the feast from which it takes its title have generally been unsuccessful: when the Duke of York's theatre company revived *Twelfth Night* on 6 January 1663, for example, Samuel Pepys was piqued by its lack of seasonal content, complaining that it was 'a silly play and not relating at all to the name or day', and the costuming and decor of the Renaissance Theatre Company's production of 1987, subsequently filmed, which replaced the garden scene's box tree with a Christmas tree and deliberately made Malvolio resemble Scrooge, didn't convince everyone.) But the title does suggest an environment in which folly enjoys just the sort of licence demanded by Feste, and so the final outcome of the fool's confrontation with Malvolio is perhaps inevitable. Malvolio is driven out of the play, exorcised like one of the spirits Feste purports to find possessing Malvolio's body, and it is Feste who remains in sole charge of the stage to sing the epilogue.

So in *Twelfth Night* we have a play which explores some often claustrophobic and self-deluding varieties of love; we hear a good deal of music, which helps to foreground an anxious preoccupation with the passing of time; and we enter a controversy over feasting and revelry, played out in a spectacularly, heartbreakingly successful practical joke. Apart from an unusually rich and self-conscious juxtaposition of these ingredients, what does the experiment in comic form that is *Twelfth Night* really amount to? One good way of gauging the real distinctiveness of this play's achievement is suggested by the very first written account of it which we have. This was provided by a perceptive and well-informed London barrister called John Manningham, who watched Shakespeare's company perform as hired entertainment at a dinner held in the hall of his Inn of Court, Middle Temple, on 2 February 1602:

At our feast we had a play called *Twelfth Night* or *What You Will*; much like the *Comedy of Errors*, or *Menaechmi* in Plautus, but most like and near to that in Italian called *Inganni*. A good practice in it to make the steward believe his lady widow was in love with him, by counterfeiting a letter as from his lady in general terms, telling him what she liked best in him, and prescribing his gesture in smiling, his apparel, etc. And then when he came to practise, making him believe they took him to be mad.

Manningham is mainly struck by two things about the play. One of them is Malvolio, whose sub-plot, wholly Shakespeare's own invention, he summarizes with remarkable thoroughness and accuracy (save for his mistake in thinking Olivia a widow, to which I'll return), so that these short notes accurately predict the extent to which the steward has been regarded as the star part of this play for much of its stage history. The other, though, is the extent to which *Twelfth Night*, however novel its sub-plot, rewrites earlier works in its genre, specifically Shakespeare's own previous play about twins *The Comedy of Errors* and its Roman source, and an Italian comedy. It's the latter which is most important as a source for *Twelfth Night*, and a quick glance at how radically Shakespeare transformed it can highlight a great deal about his purposes in designing this play.

By '*Inganni*' Manningham meant *Gl'Ingannati* (*The Deceived*), an anonymous play performed in Siena in 1531; Shakespeare probably never saw it in the original Italian, but by his time it had already spawned a number of accessible derivatives. A prose version by Matteo Bandello appears in his immense collection of prose romances, the *Novelle* (1554–73), and this was translated into French by François de Belleforest as one of his *Histoires tragiques* (1559–82). Shakespeare may have known Bandello's Italian version, and he certainly knew Belleforest's book, from which he took the story of *Hamlet* at around the same time as he was writing *Twelfth Night*. He probably knew an English translation of Belleforest too, Geoffrey Fenton's *Certain Tragical Discourses* (1567), but the prose descendant of *Gl'Ingannati* which Shakespeare knew best was a story called 'Apolonius and Silla', adapted from the Bandello–Belleforest version by an ex-soldier called Barnabe Rich and told as the second story in his book *Farewell to Military Profession* (1581). Shakespeare had already borrowed from this story when writing an earlier play about a girl who follows her beloved disguised as a page, *The Two Gentlemen of Verona* (c. 1590, a play which tries out a number of motifs which find their fullest development in *Twelfth Night*), but this time his dramatization would be both more thorough and more revealing.

To come to 'Apolonius and Silla' from the play Shakespeare made of it is immediately to find oneself in a simpler, narrower and more extroverted world. Its heroine, Silla (the original for Viola but at first considerably less passive), is the daughter of Pontus, Duke of Cyprus, with whom Apolonius, the Duke of Constantinople (an altogether more vigorous figure than his descendant, Orsino), stays for a while on his way home from a crusade against the Turks. During this stay, Silla falls in love with Apolonius, so violently that after his departure she follows him in secret, accompanied only by her faithful servant Pedro. They book a passage on a ship towards Constantinople, which is shipwrecked only just in time to prevent its at first friendly captain from raping Silla; both he and Pedro are among the drowned, but Silla comes safely ashore and, determined to avoid any such future unpleasantness, she continues towards Constantinople dressed as a man and calling herself by her brother's name, Silvio. In this disguise she obtains service with Apolonius, but he is in love with a local widow, the Lady Julina (the original for Olivia, as Manningham was perhaps recognizing when he accidentally described Olivia as a widow), and he sends 'Silvio' to woo her on his behalf. Julina falls in love with this reluctant love-messenger, and when the real Silvio arrives in Constantinople looking for his fugitive sister she chances to meet him and eagerly invites him to supper. Although a little alarmed by the suddenness of her interest, Silvio goes to Julina's house, where he not only has supper but sleeps with her afterwards. In the morning, however, he leaves for the provinces to continue searching for Silla. In response to Apolonius's continuing solicitations, Julina tells him that he should desist because she has promised herself in marriage to another, and the Duke gathers from the talk of servants that his successful rival is Silvio: furious, he confines Silla in a dungeon. Worried by Silvio's absence, especially when she finds herself to be pregnant, Julina hears that he is under lock and key, and goes to Apolonius: the Duke is still more enraged to learn that his once-trusted page has even impregnated his beloved, and he has Silla brought into their presence. Both are aghast when Silla denies all knowledge of the betrothal, and they accuse her of perjury in a scene which occupies much of the tale's length. Silla is at last forced to prove to Julina that she is not the father of the unborn child by taking her aside and revealing what is called the 'impediment' that renders this impossible:

'. . . although I could allege many reasons to prove my sayings true, yet I refer myself to the experience and bounty of your mind.' And herewithal loosing his garments down to his stomach, ['Silvio'] showed Julina his breasts and pretty teats, surmounting far the whiteness of snow itself, saying: 'Lo, madam, behold here the party whom you have challenged to be the father of your child. See, I am a woman, the daughter of a noble duke, who only for the love of him whom you so lightly have shaken off have forsaken my father, abandoned my country, and in manner as you see am become a serving man . . .'

Julina is both baffled and dismayed, and shuts herself up from the world in shame, but when Apolonius learns Silla's real identity he is deeply moved that she has undergone such trials in pursuit of his love, and he at once proposes: soon they enjoy a magnificent public wedding. The news of this wedding, fortunately, reaches Silvio, who returns to Constantinople to be reunited with his newly married sister. Suitably abashed to hear about what has happened to Julina, he confides all that passed between them to Apolonius. Apolonius takes Silvio to the grieving Julina, where he begs her forgiveness. She is so happy that at first she thinks she is dreaming, and they too marry, 'and thus Silvio having attained a noble wife, and Silla his sister her desired husband, they passed the residue of their days with such delight, as those that have accomplished the perfection of their felicities'.

There are a number of minor details in this story
which, though left out by Shakespeare, still faintly haunt
the play as it stands: for example, although in *Twelfth
Night* the captain of the ship, unlike his counterpart in
the prose romance, survives the wreck and helps the
heroine, Viola seems dimly to remember his avatar in
'Apolonius and Silla', pausing before deciding that in his
case his professed friendship is genuine (1.2.48–52). It is
as if the sea captain, in Shakespeare's hands, has been
conflated with another casualty of Rich's storm, the
faithful Pedro, who perhaps also contributed something
to Antonio (though Antonio also owes a good deal to
another of Shakespeare's selfless, earnest and unmarried
male friends, the Antonio of *The Merchant of Venice*).
What is more striking, though, and what obliged
Manningham to invoke *The Comedy of Errors* and
Menaechmi as additional sources for *Twelfth Night*, is that
'Apolonius and Silla' isn't actually a story about twins,
and never raises the possibility that the heroine's brother
might be dead. Although the *Gl'Ingannati* plot depends
on a close physical resemblance between Silla and Silvio,
Rich doesn't specify that they are twins (explaining their
likeness only by the fact that Silla was Silvio's 'natural
sister, both by father and mother'), and this aspect of
'Apolonius and Silla' perhaps lingers in *Twelfth Night*
when the reunited Viola and Sebastian mutually confirm
their identities by remembering that their father died
'that day when Viola from her birth | Had numbered
thirteen years' (V.1.241–2). The odd phrasing of this
remark of Viola's apparently overlooks the fact that this
must have been Sebastian's thirteenth birthday too, an
oversight which few real twins, surely, would commit;
even Sebastian refers to what ought to be his own birthday
only as 'That day that made my sister thirteen years'

(V.1.245). Otherwise, though, for Shakespeare this is emphatically a scene about twinship ('An apple cleft in two is not more twin | Than these two creatures' (220–21), declares Antonio), and the reunion of the identical brother and sister provides the emotional climax of *Twelfth Night* in a way for which Rich's story – where the emphasis is far more squarely on getting the couples together than on rejoining the siblings – does nothing to prepare us. What little we hear of the reunion in Rich is much more concerned with the new family relation between Silvio and Apolonius: 'coming to his sister he was joyfully received, and most lovingly welcomed, and entertained of the Duke, his brother-in-law'. It isn't simply that Shakespeare combines the last two major scenes of Rich's tale, so that the reproaching of the apparently faithless page is cut short by the unexpected and clarifying arrival of the brother; it's that for Shakespeare the miraculous and to the onlookers uncanny restoration of the twins to one another lifts the scene to a pitch of wonder and joy which the play's betrothals never really approach. Why? Shakespeare knew perfectly well that this plot was in one sense impossible (as his half-admission that these siblings don't really share a birthday almost betrays), since in nature truly identical twins are only ever of the same sex, but for him it may have dramatized an impossible personal fantasy anyway. He himself was the father of twins, Judith and Hamnet, but the boy had died five years before this play was written, at the age of eleven. (It is an odd minor coincidence that John Manningham saw *Twelfth Night* on the seventeenth anniversary of the twins' christening.) In the play, if not in life, the dead twin brother comes back to life, having been preserved in the meantime through the sister's resemblance to him: 'I my brother know | Yet living in my glass', says Viola (III.4.370–71). It may seem sentimental to import this biographical detail into a consideration of *Twelfth Night*, but it's at very least striking that the writer of this greatest of all comedies about separated twins should have felt compelled to adapt it from a story which isn't about twins at all. In Rich's story, the events leading up to and including the ship-wreck are simply the pretext for the heroine to assume male disguise; in *Twelfth Night* the loss and rediscovery of the brother frame and complete the entire plot.

With this much emphasis on the moving reunion between the siblings, love, in Shakespeare's play as opposed to Rich's story, isn't confined to sexual love; and equally sexual love isn't confined to its reproductive function. Just as striking as Shakespeare's introduction of twinship and the shadow of death into his plot is his dele-tion of pregnancy. Rich's sense that his cross-dressed heroine is to most intents and purposes simply a man with an 'impediment' to male fertility survives in *Twelfth Night* as Viola's sense of impotence when obliged to draw a sword against Sir Andrew ('A little thing would make me tell them how much I lack of a man', III.4.293–4), and indeed in the form of her assumed name. She initially proposes to be presented to Orsino as a eunuch, and her alias, Cesario, literally means 'cut', although Shakespeare seems to forget this detail in the excitement of her subse-quent scenes with the nonetheless infatuated Olivia. But then perhaps fertility isn't the point of love in this play anyway, marking another radical departure from Shakespeare's earlier comedies. Unlike Benedick in *Much Ado About Nothing*, who self-sacrificingly reconciles himself to courting Beatrice on the grounds that 'the world must be peopled' (II.3.234–5), or Rosalind in *As You Like It*, who first betrays the seriousness of her interest in Orlando by jokingly referring to him as 'my child's father' (I.3.11), the young lovers in *Twelfth Night* are strictly interested in love as a mode of personal fulfilment rather than as a means towards procreation, for just as this play diverges from Rich in its lack of an older generation so it also lacks any very wholehearted gestures towards posterity ('What is love? 'Tis not hereafter; | Present mirth hath present laughter', as Feste's song argues, II.3.45–6). It is true that Viola, wooing Olivia on Orsino's behalf in Act I, scene 5, urges her, conventionally enough, not to miss the opportunity to reproduce, so that the world may still have living embodiments of her beauty in the form of children after her death: 'Lady, you are the cruellest she alive, | If you will lead these graces to the grave, | And leave the world no copy' (I.5.230–32). This is just the argument Shakespeare had earlier deployed in the first batch of his Sonnets, composed around 1593, poems which seem to have been designed to persuade an aristocratic youth to marry and beget children, and which may in that instance have been dramatically over-successful: their likeliest addressee, Shakespeare's patron the Earl of Southampton, impregnated and married one of Queen Elizabeth's ladies-in-waiting in 1595 and was imprisoned in the Fleet as a result. But it doesn't work on Olivia, who despite her mourning veil seems far more interested in enjoying her own beauty now than in propagating it for the future. Unlike the fertile Julina, she flippantly replies that she will simply have her charms catalogued instead, disseminating them not sexually but textually:

> O sir, I will not be so hard-hearted. I will give out divers schedules of my beauty. It shall be inventoried, and every particle and utensil labelled to my will. As, item: two lips,

indifferent red; item: two grey eyes, with lids to them; item: one neck, one chin, and so forth. (II.5.233–7)

Surprisingly, the subject of child-bearing never arises again, not even at a conclusion which might otherwise seem to be all about cementing dynastic marriages. Olivia arranges for her marriage with Sebastian, who she still thinks is Cesario, to be kept secret for the time being in Act IV, scene 3 without the possibility of pregnancy ever being discussed, and in the following scene Viola's projected wedding to Orsino is not envisaged as her transformation into a matriarchal duchess but merely the ratification of her abrupt promotion to what has hitherto been Olivia's position as the nominal object of his amorous fixation. After Viola gets her women's clothes back, the Duke tells her, she will become 'Orsino's mistress, and his fancy's queen' (V.1.385), and neither of these titles seems to imagine motherhood as a very urgent priority. In *Twelfth Night* the empirical biology of sexual difference isn't allowed to trump all else, and while Rich's story is primarily about two heterosexual couples moving towards marriage, Shakespeare both interrupts that progress – Viola can't even get her clothes back, so that Orsino is still calling her 'Cesario' and 'boy' to the end of the play – and juxtaposes it with all sorts of relationships which either don't lead to marriage or never sought to in the first place. Among the most intense scenes of *Twelfth Night*, as we've seen, are those between two women, Viola and Olivia, whose unusual affinity is only confirmed by the virtually anagrammatic names Shakespeare gives them; Orsino is already so close to his page boy Cesario that the revelation that he is really a girl at the end of the play doesn't present any insurmountable problems to the future course of their relationship; and Antonio's adoration of Sebastian (who, when we first meet them, has been living with him for three months under the alias of 'Roderigo') is sufficiently powerful to make him risk his life on his beloved's behalf. In all of these complete alterations to his source, Shakespeare is apparently at pains to keep Illyria sexually plural, and the play's willingness to acknowledge the homoerotic can't be explained solely by the fact that he was writing for an all-male company in which women were played by boys. (Surviving eyewitness testimony by Elizabethan and Jacobean theatregoers, in any case, suggests that this convention was all but invisible to audiences perfectly willing to accept it, as it still can be in Japanese kabuki theatre, where women's roles may be played by naturalistic female impersonators called *onna-gata*.) Just as *Twelfth Night* isn't all unmitigated comedy, so it isn't all about the happy ending conventionally represented by marriage – and the ending of this play, provisional and full of 'ifs' and almost broken off by the vengeful last appearance of Malvolio, is as conspicuous for its losers as it is for any perfection of felicity guaranteed to its winners. Malvolio doesn't get Olivia, and nor does Orsino, and nor does Sir Andrew, who is even spurned by his supposed friend Sir Toby; Olivia doesn't get Cesario (unlike her counterpart in Rich, who thought she was wooing Silvio and gets Silvio); Antonio, apparently forgotten for the last 200 lines of the play, is parted from Sebastian; and even if Viola gets her dead brother back, Olivia doesn't get hers. And Feste, the fool who has triumphed over Malvolio, is left all on his own on the stage and not paired off with anyone; but, as if convinced that music may be the food of love, he plays on:

When that I was and a little tiny boy,
  With hey-ho, the wind and the rain;
A foolish thing was but a toy,
  For the rain it raineth every day. (V.1.386–9)

The pleasures and possibilities offered by *Twelfth Night*, then, traverse an extraordinary range: it can provide romantic adventure, painfully funny jokes, minutely observed social comedy, glimpses of religious conflict, unabashed lyricism, and a close-focus view of personal relationships that seems if anything even more to the point in our own affluent society, in which contraception and pluralism have at once expanded the acceptable scope of sexuality and potentially trivialized it, than the play must have seemed in 1601. It is only fitting that *Twelfth Night* should end, reflectively, in music, as its fool collapses the entire history of the universe into local weather conditions and a welcome promise that this show will go on again, as by now it has been going on for four centuries:

A great while ago the world began,
  With hey-ho, the wind and the rain;
But that's all one, our play is done,
  And we'll strive to please you every day
                                  (V.1.402–5)

Michael Dobson

The Play in Performance

Despite the potential complications posed by the need for something that Sir Toby, Sir Andrew and Fabian can hide behind in the garden scene, Act II, scene 5 (nominally a box tree), *Twelfth Night* is in practical terms a comparatively simple play to stage. As Manningham's enjoyment of the play at his Inn of Court feast demonstrates, it can readily be adapted for performance in front of an undecorated screen with two entrance doorways, and the play's tricks with our sense of which actor is Viola and which is Sebastian are, if anything, enhanced if there are only two doors; one twin can leave through one just before the other enters through the other (as at the transition between Act II, scenes 1 and 2), leaving us momentarily uncertain as to whether we are seeing a re-entry or a fresh entrance. Hypothetical reconstructions of Elizabethan styles and methods of performance have in fact been a recurrent feature of the play's stage history, as if the nostalgia indulged by Orsino over the melody of 'Come away, come away, death' were contagious. William Poel, whose semi-professional Elizabethan Stage Society pioneered attempts at playing Shakespeare's plays using 'authentic' sixteenth-century methods, produced the play twice, in 1897 and in 1903, and more recently it has twice been revived at its earliest recorded venue, the

hall at Middle Temple. In 1951 a Tudor-dress production
of *Twelfth Night* celebrated the hall's restoration after the
damage it had suffered in the Blitz, and in February 2002
an all-male production by Mark Rylance's company from
Shakespeare's Globe Theatre marked the 400th anniver-
sary of Manningham's feast by again mounting the play
there in Elizabethan style (even if its gestures towards
historical authenticity were a little compromised by the
fact that the female roles were played by adults rather
than boys: Rylance himself made a memorably dignified
Olivia). One of the most famous productions of modern
times, while less consciously antiquarian than either of
these Middle Temple experiments, also chose an
Elizabethan design and costumes, its simple, sparse set
dominated by a tunnel-like Tudor long gallery running
upstage: this was John Barton's RSC production of 1969,
which opened at the Royal Shakespeare Theatre in
Stratford and subsequently toured extensively, with Judi
Dench as Viola and Donald Sinden as Malvolio.

Barton's production was described as 'autumnal' and
'melancholy', achieving a '*fin-de-siècle*' or 'Chekhovian'
quality, and in this respect it was perhaps more characteristic of its time than in its choice of period. Productions
of *Twelfth Night* have often been nostalgic, but since the
1950s it has been much more common for English productions to look wistfully back not to Shakespeare's time but
to the pre-war era of the country house, with Malvolio
costumed less as an Elizabethan steward than as an
Edwardian or inter-war butler and Sir Toby and Sir
Andrew dressed so as to resemble characters from
Kenneth Grahame's *Toad of Toad Hall* or P. G.
Wodehouse's Jeeves stories. Prominent examples would
include Sam Mendes's award-winning revival at the
Donmar Warehouse in 2002, with Simon Russell Beale

as a preening Malvolio, and Trevor Nunn's film version
of 1996. Certainly one of the benefits of placing the play's
action nearer to the present day is that the costuming,
rather than producing a rather generic sense of olde-
worlde fancy dress, can render the social distinctions so
important for this play's below-stairs sub-plot much more
comprehensibly visible. The difficulty comes with the
cross-gartering and the yellow stockings, which seem
much less likely fashions for Olivia to request Malvolio
to adopt in an age when gentlemen wear long trousers
rather than doublet and hose: some modern-dress
Malvolios have even had kilts thrust upon them (for
Malvolio read MacVolio?), though others (such as
Russell Beale) have managed hilariously enough by
gesturing enigmatically and misunderstandably down-
wards towards yellow socks while walking as though some
obscure species of suspenders were killing them.

If Illyria has often looked like either Elizabethan or
Edwardian England, some directors have preferred to
stress its potential exoticism. Dorothea Jordan's famous
Viola, in the Regency period, clad herself as Cesario
in a dashing Ottoman turban, and this element of
Orientalism has survived in more recent productions:
Ariane Mnouchkine's eclectic Parisian *Nuit des rois* of
1982 combined Indian and Persian designs with Asian
theatrical conventions, unsettling familiar expectations
about the Western tradition of romantic love, and in Tim
Supple's 1997 production at the Young Vic in London
(the basis for his subsequent television film of 2003)
Viola and Sebastian were glamorously silk-clad refugees
from the Indian subcontinent. Bill Alexander's RSC
production of 1987 perhaps took its Illyria most literally,
showing a Greek society in which Malvolio (Antony Sher)
looked like an Orthodox cleric; at the other end of the

spectrum, Harley Granville-Barker's at the Savoy in 1912 pioneered a more stylized, non-realist setting. But wherever and whenever directors place Illyria, its realization has generally been dominated by a sense of Olivia's house and garden, which in the Victorian and early-twentieth-century era of the picture-frame stage were often rendered as such substantial and detailed sets that Shakespeare's text had to be reordered so as to minimize the number of set changes required. Herbert Beerbohm Tree's production of 1901, for example, gave Olivia's elaborately terraced garden real grass and fountains, requiring all the scenes set there to be run consecutively, and as recently as 1987 the Renaissance Theatre Company's Christmassy production (subsequently filmed) reused its elaborate mock-up of the snowbound garden in front of a Victorian mansion as the unlikely setting for the catch scene, Act II, scene 3, into which Richard Briers' Malvolio emerged grim and shivering in a long white nightshirt.

It is not incidental that the character I have had most occasion to mention so far has been Malvolio, since his has stood out as the prime male role in *Twelfth Night* ever since Manningham first noted down his plot in 1602. In the 1630s, King Charles I wrote 'Malvolio' next to the play's title in his copy of the Shakespeare Folio, and the steward's pre-Civil War popularity is further attested in the dedicatory poem contributed by Leonard Digges to an edition of Shakespeare's poems in 1640: '. . . lo, in a trice | The Cockpit galleries, boxes, all are full | To hear Malvolio, that cross-gartered gull.' Although the play went out of fashion in the later seventeenth century, its aura of romance and poetry dismissed as implausible and escapist (so that in 1703 it was even rewritten, mainly in prose, as Charles Burnaby's *Love Betrayed; or,*

The Agreeable Disappointment), *Twelfth Night* returned triumphantly to the repertory in 1741 with the great Charles Macklin as Malvolio, and a succession of star actors and actor-managers have been competing for the part ever since, from Richard Yates through Henry Irving (who hugged himself, weeping with joy, on being convinced of Olivia's love) down to Laurence Olivier, who played the role at Stratford in John Gielgud's Jacobean-dress production of 1955. Olivier, who wore explicitly Puritan clothes, stressed the steward's upward mobility and his outsider status (resembling, according to some observers, an effeminate Jewish hairdresser); his was a young, oily Malvolio, as opposed to an old, cold one (examples of the latter school have included John Lowe, Alec Guinness, Nigel Hawthorne, Oliver Cotton and Philip Voss). The role of Feste, too, probably written for the gifted actor-musician Robert Armin, has sometimes been played as young and impish, sometimes old and saturnine, varying from Anton Lesser's wild-eyed gipsy-like bohemian (1987) to David Hargreaves' wry, white-bearded lamenter of lost youth (in Bill Alexander's production, 2001).

Ever since professional actresses were first allowed to appear on the English stage in the 1660s, the most conspicuous role for a woman in the play has been Viola, and the combination of professed bashful modesty with the ample display of leg afforded by Cesario's breeches made her a special favourite with eighteenth- and nineteenth-century audiences: Dorothea Jordan, Charlotte Cushman and Ellen Terry were especially well received. Hannah Pritchard and Kitty Clive, who had a close comic rapport, were the first smash-hit Viola and Olivia in 1741, and the scenes between the page and the lady have often seemed the heart of the play, as in Peter Hall's gauzy 1958 production, in which Geraldine McEwan's willowy Olivia yearned for Dorothy Tutin's petite Viola. It's worth pointing out that despite the need for Cesario to look like a plausible male mate for Olivia, Violas have often been small and bird-like: one of the role's greatest players was Judi Dench in 1969, and in the BBC television version of 1980 Viola was played by the kittenish sitcom specialist Felicity Kendal. The sense that Viola is the focal character of the play is reflected by one reordering of scenes which is still frequently followed by present-day productions, by which the play is made to open with Viola's arrival in Illyria rather than Orsino's invocation of music: this significantly alters the play, since it makes Illyria into something that happens to Viola rather than vice versa, but stage-managerial considerations have often made it convenient. It is characteristic of the play that the two glorious roles of Malvolio and Viola each provide enormous scope for theatrical interpretation and each demand an enormous range of technique, moving as they do between outright farce and the subtlest shades of pathos.

Different handlings of the reunion between Viola and her brother in Act V have also varied widely in tone. Some producers have reduced the reunion to the anticlimactic end of an irrelevant theatrical trick by using the same performer to play Viola and Sebastian, a ploy pioneered in the theatre by the actress Kate Terry in 1865 (presumably with the help of a double and some rewriting in Act V), and pursued more practically on the screen, with equally dulling effect, by Yakow Frid's Russian film of 1955 (with Katya Luchko) and John Dexter's television version of 1970 (with Joan Plowright). Others have sought, more sensitively, to alternate the joy of the reunion with incidental pieces of comic business. In the Globe company's 2002 production at Middle Temple, for

example, Orsino was unable to recognize which twin was
his page, initially propositioning Sebastian by mistake on
'Boy, thou hast said to me a thousand times . . .' (V.1.264),
to his comical discomfiture. Others again have gone for
laughs at all costs, a flattening strategy well exemplified
by the tendency among recent Olivias (such as Helen
McCrory in Sam Mendes's 2002 production) to play her
exclamation on seeing the twins together, 'Most
wonderful!' (V.1.222), as if it merely expressed a sala-
cious delight at having apparently married a self-cloning
prodigy able to service her either in a threesome or in
shifts.

  The play, despite its interest in music and what some
critics have described as its Mozartian qualities, has never
been set as a full-scale opera, although its musical content
has varied considerably over time in other ways.
Eighteenth- and nineteenth-century productions tended
to reassign Feste's two love-lyrics to Viola (a practice
recorded, for example, by Helena Modjeska's performance edition of 1883), or, if neither the Viola nor the
Feste was a good singer, to cut them both: 'O mistress
mine' and 'Come away, come away, death' are wholly
absent from the acting text used by Dorothea Jordan and
published by Elizabeth Inchbald in 1808, though the catch
scene acquires two new musical additions, 'Christmas
comes but once a year' and 'Which is the properest day
to drink?'. Settings of Feste's songs have varied between
adaptations or pastiches of Elizabethan melodies, speci-
mens of contemporary song (such as the famous 1741
settings by Thomas Arne), or, more recently, attempts
to identify Feste with modern youth culture. The play
was heavily adapted as a rock opera, *Your Own Thing*,
in America in 1968, and Feste has been armed with an
electric guitar in a number of modern-dress revivals of

Shakespeare's original since, such as Lucy Bailey's at the Royal Exchange in Manchester in 2003.

In common with a peculiar American film adaptation of 1972, directed by Ron Wertheim, Bailey's production played Orsino as a fading rock star, and both of these accounts of the play took considerable interest in the play's potential for homoerotic readings, which have been as prominent over the last quarter-century of perform-ances of *Twelfth Night* as they have been in the same period's literary criticism. Cheek by Jowl's watershed production of 1986, for example, directed by Declan Donellan, made something of a joke of this, playing Act III, scene 3 as though Sebastian wanted to conceal the fact that his relationship with Antonio was actively gay from the audience but Antonio wanted to 'out' him: after the giggling way in which Antonio underlined their rendezvous at the Elephant, 'There shall you have me' (43), Sebastian gave up the struggle. More often Antonio has been played as homosexual but Sebastian only dimly aware of the nature of his feelings, but it is nowadays increasingly rare to see a production of *Twelfth Night* in which Orsino doesn't kiss Cesario, or in which the sexual dimension to Olivia's interest in Viola disappears alto-gether once she learns that she is female. The play continues richly to insinuate itself into our own society's understandings of love, and when performers lose an interest in reinterpreting its immense scope of possible meanings and moods it probably won't be worth going to the theatre any more anyway.

Michael Dobson

Further Reading

EDITIONS

Major scholarly editions of *Twelfth Night*, all conveniently available in paperback, are the Oxford, edited by Stanley Wells and Roger Warren (1994); the Arden, edited by J. M. Lothian and T. W. Craik (1975); and the New Cambridge, edited by Elizabeth Story Donno (1985, re-issued with a new introduction by Penny Gay, 2004). The definitive essay on its text remains R. K. Turner's 'The Text of *Twelfth Night*', *Shakespeare Quarterly* 26 (1975), which convincingly argues that the first edition of the play, in the 1623 Folio, was set from a playhouse transcript of Shakespeare's own manuscript.

BACKGROUND MATERIAL

The scholarly editions cited above reprint much of Rich's 'Apolonius and Silla', as does Bruce R. Smith's edition of the play, *'Twelfth Night': Texts and Contexts* (2001), in the Bedford Shakespeare series, which also supplies a considerable further archive of contemporary documents on the play's cultural and theatrical contexts. 'Apolonius and Silla' also appears in T. J. B. Spencer's collection

Elizabethan Love Stories (1968). The fullest discussion of the play's sources and analogues remains that of Geoffrey Bullough, in volume II of his *Narrative and Dramatic Sources of Shakespeare* (1957–75), while recent contributions to this discussion include A. B. Taylor, 'Shakespeare Rewriting Ovid: Olivia's Interview with Viola and the Narcissus Myth', *Shakespeare Survey 50* (1997).

CRITICISM

Possibly the most influential book on Shakespearian comedy of the last half century, C. L. Barber's *Shakespeare's Festive Comedy* (1959), which examines Shakespeare's favourite genre from a broadly anthropological perspective, remains essential reading: its chapter on *Twelfth Night* is usefully reprinted in Stanley Wells's collection *'Twelfth Night': Critical Essays* (1986), along with important essays by A. C. Bradley, Harry Levin, Harold Jenkins, L. G. Salingar, A. S. Leggatt, John Russell Brown, Karen Greif, Ralph Berry and Jorg Hasler. Critical approaches to the genre as a whole are usefully surveyed in Alexander Leggatt (ed.), *The Cambridge Companion to Shakespearean Comedy* (2002), which includes a good essay on *Twelfth Night* by Barbara Hodgdon, and in Jean Howard and Richard Dutton (eds.), *The Blackwell Companions to Shakespeare: The Comedies* (2003), which includes another by Penny Gay. Further perspectives on the play are gathered in R. S. White (ed.), *New Casebooks: 'Twelfth Night'* (1996). Useful general treatments include Anne Barton's '*As You Like It* and *Twelfth Night*: Shakespeare's Sense of an Ending', which is given in part in Wells's *'Twelfth Night': Critical Essays* and in full in D. J. Palmer and M.

Bradbury's *Shakespearean Comedy* (1972) as well as in Barton's own *Essays, Mainly Shakespearean* (1994); Barbara Everett's 'Or What You Will', *Essays in Criticism* 35 (1985); M. C. Bradbrook's discussion of its musical fool in *Shakespeare the Craftsman* (1968); and Stevie Davies's *William Shakespeare: 'Twelfth Night'* (Penguin Critical Studies, 1993).

Much recent criticism of the play has concentrated on its depictions of gender and sexuality. Important contextualizing work here includes Valerie Traub's essay 'Gender and Sexuality in Shakespeare', in Margreta de Grazia and Stanley Wells (eds.), *The Cambridge Companion to Shakespeare* (2001), while Traub looks more closely at *Twelfth Night* and the homoerotic in *Desire and Anxiety: Circulations of Sexuality in Shakespearean Drama* (1992). Other important work in this field includes Michael Shapiro, *Gender in Play on the Shakespearean Stage* (1996), Bruce R. Smith, *Homosexual Desire in Shakespeare's England: A Cultural Poetics* (1991) and Stephen Orgel, *Impersonations: The Performance of Gender in Renaissance England* (1996), which synthesizes and interrogates a good deal of earlier work on cross-dressing and the boy actor. Matthew Wikander's article '"As sweet as maidenhead": The Profession of the Boy-Actress in *Twelfth Night*' is also of interest, in *Comparative Drama*, 20 (1986–7). A widely read and contentious essay on the play's representations of sexual difference remains Stephen Greenblatt's 'Fiction and Friction', in his *Shakespearean Negotiations* (1988).

On twinship in the play, Janice Wardle's essay '*Twelfth Night*: "One face, one voice, one habit, and two persons!"' appears in Deborah Cartmell and Michael Scott (eds.), *Talking Shakespeare* (2001), and John M. Mercer considers 'Twin Relationships in Shakespeare' in *The Upstart Crow*

9 (1989). The topic of service in *Twelfth Night* is discussed by Mark Thornton Burnett in his *Masters and Servants in English Renaissance Drama and Culture* (1997), and is related to the play's perspectives on gender in Lisa Jardine's *Reading Shakespeare Historically* (1996). Treatments of Malvolio in particular include Stephen Booth's '*Twelfth Night* I.i: Malvolio as Audience', in Paul Erickson and Coppélia Kahn (eds.), *Shakespeare's Rough Magic: Essays in Honour of C. L. Barber* (1985), and Marjorie Garber's post-structuralist account of the puzzling anagram posed in Maria's forged letter, in her *Shakespeare's Ghost Writers* (1987). Another widely read post-structuralist essay on the play is Geoffrey H. Hartmann's 'Shakespeare's Poetical Character in *Twelfth Night*', in *Shakespeare and the Question of Theory*, ed. Patricia Parker and Geoffrey Hartmann (1985).

THE PLAY IN PERFORMANCE

The play's original staging, both at the Globe and at Middle Temple, is discussed by Peter Thomson in *Shakespeare's Theatre* (1983) and by John H. Astington in 'Malvolio and the Dark House', *Shakespeare Survey 41* (1989). It is also considered by T. J. King in *Shakespearean Staging, 1599–1642* (1971), and King's conclusions are further refined by Tim Fitzpatrick, 'Stage Management, Dramaturgy and Spatial Semiotics in Shakespeare's Dialogue', *Theatre Research International* 23, 1 (1999). Leslie Hotson attempted to argue that the play was first performed on Twelfth Night in 1601 in his *The First Night of 'Twelfth Night'* (1954), which remains valuable if ultimately unconvincing. General studies of the play's performance history include Lois Potter, *Text*

and Performance: 'Twelfth Night' (1985) and Laurie E.
Osborne's combination of stage history and post-
structuralist reading, *The Trick of Singularity: 'Twelfth
Night' and the Performance Editions* (1996). The late-
twentieth-century emergence of Antonio as an explicitly
homosexual role is discussed in Stanley Wells's *Looking
for Sex in Shakespeare* (2004). Some of the most illumi-
nating writing about the play's fortunes and possibilities
in performance has been published by theatre profes-
sionals: it includes Michael Billington's collection of inter-
views with directors in *Approaches to 'Twelfth Night'*, in
the Directors' Shakespeare series (1990; this also includes
a full stage history of the play), Emma Fielding's
Actors on Shakespeare: 'Twelfth Night' (2002), Michael
Pennington's *'Twelfth Night': A User's Guide* (2000),
Donald Sinden's essay 'Malvolio in *Twelfth Night*', in
Philip Brockbank (ed.), *Players of Shakespeare 1* (1985),
Zoe Wanamaker's 'Viola in *Twelfth Night*', in Russell
Jackson and Robert Smallwood (eds.), *Players of
Shakespeare 2* (1988), and Zoe Waites and Matilda
Ziegler's 'Viola and Olivia in *Twelfth Night*', in Robert
Smallwood (ed.), *Players of Shakespeare 5* (2003).

TWELFTH NIGHT,
OR WHAT YOU WILL

The Characters in the Play

ORSINO, Duke of Illyria
VALENTINE ⎫ gentlemen attending on Orsino
CURIO   ⎭
FIRST OFFICER
SECOND OFFICER

VIOLA, a shipwrecked lady, later disguised as Cesario
SEBASTIAN, her twin brother
CAPTAIN of the wrecked ship
ANTONIO, another sea captain

OLIVIA, a countess
MARIA, her waiting-gentlewoman
SIR TOBY Belch, her uncle
SIR ANDREW Aguecheek, Sir Toby's protégé
MALVOLIO, Olivia's steward
FABIAN, a member of her household
FESTE, her jester
A PRIEST
A SERVANT

Musicians, lords, sailors, attendants

Music. Enter Orsino Duke of Illyria, Curio, and
other lords

ORSINO

If music be the food of love, play on,
Give me excess of it, that, surfeiting,
The appetite may sicken, and so die.
That strain again! It had a dying fall.
O, it came o'er my ear like the sweet sound
That breathes upon a bank of violets,
Stealing and giving odour. Enough, no more!
'Tis not so sweet now as it was before.
O spirit of love, how quick and fresh art thou,
That, notwithstanding thy capacity   10
Receiveth as the sea, naught enters there,
Of what validity and pitch soe'er,
But falls into abatement and low price
Even in a minute. So full of shapes is fancy
That it alone is high fantastical.

CURIO

Will you go hunt, my lord?

ORSINO

What, Curio?

CURIO

The hart.

ORSINO
    Why, so I do, the noblest that I have.
20   O, when mine eyes did see Olivia first,
    Methought she purged the air of pestilence.
    That instant was I turned into a hart,
    And my desires, like fell and cruel hounds,
    E'er since pursue me.
       Enter Valentine

                    How now! What news from her?

VALENTINE
    So please my lord, I might not be admitted,
    But from her handmaid do return this answer:
    The element itself, till seven years' heat,
    Shall not behold her face at ample view,
    But like a cloistress she will veilèd walk,
30   And water once a day her chamber round
    With eye-offending brine; all this to season
    A brother's dead love, which she would keep fresh
    And lasting, in her sad remembrance.

ORSINO
    O, she that hath a heart of that fine frame
    To pay this debt of love but to a brother –
    How will she love, when the rich golden shaft
    Hath killed the flock of all affections else
    That live in her; when liver, brain, and heart,
    These sovereign thrones, are all supplied and filled –
40   Her sweet perfections – with one self king!
    Away before me to sweet beds of flowers!
    Love thoughts lie rich when canopied with bowers.
                          Exeunt

I.2   *Enter Viola, a Captain, and sailors*
VIOLA
    What country, friends, is this?

CAPTAIN
This is Illyria, lady.

VIOLA
And what should I do in Illyria?
My brother, he is in Elysium.
Perchance he is not drowned. What think you, sailors?

CAPTAIN
It is perchance that you yourself were saved.

VIOLA
O, my poor brother! and so perchance may he be.

CAPTAIN
True, madam, and to comfort you with chance,
Assure yourself, after our ship did split,
When you and those poor number saved with you   10
Hung on our driving boat, I saw your brother,
Most provident in peril, bind himself —
Courage and hope both teaching him the practice —
To a strong mast, that lived upon the sea;
Where, like Arion on the dolphin's back,
I saw him hold acquaintance with the waves
So long as I could see.

VIOLA
For saying so, there's gold.
Mine own escape unfoldeth to my hope,
Whereto thy speech serves for authority,   20
The like of him. Knowest thou this country?

CAPTAIN
Ay, madam, well, for I was bred and born
Not three hours' travel from this very place.

VIOLA
Who governs here?

CAPTAIN
A noble duke, in nature as in name.

VIOLA
What is his name?

CAPTAIN
  Orsino.
VIOLA
  Orsino . . . I have heard my father name him.
  He was a bachelor then.
CAPTAIN
30 And so is now, or was so, very late;
  For but a month ago I went from hence,
  And then 'twas fresh in murmur — as you know,
  What great ones do, the less will prattle of —
  That he did seek the love of fair Olivia.
VIOLA
  What's she?
CAPTAIN
  A virtuous maid, the daughter of a count
  That died some twelvemonth since, then leaving her
  In the protection of his son, her brother,
  Who shortly also died; for whose dear love,
40 They say, she hath abjured the sight
  And company of men.
VIOLA
  O, that I served that lady,
  And might not be delivered to the world —
  Till I had made mine own occasion mellow —
  What my estate is.
CAPTAIN   That were hard to compass,
  Because she will admit no kind of suit,
  No, not the Duke's.
VIOLA
  There is a fair behaviour in thee, Captain,
  And though that nature with a beauteous wall
50 Doth oft close in pollution, yet of thee
  I will believe thou hast a mind that suits

With this thy fair and outward character.
I prithee – and I'll pay thee bounteously –
Conceal me what I am, and be my aid
For such disguise as haply shall become
The form of my intent. I'll serve this Duke.
Thou shalt present me as an eunuch to him.
It may be worth thy pains, for I can sing
And speak to him in many sorts of music
That will allow me very worth his service.   60
What else may hap to time I will commit.
Only shape thou thy silence to my wit.

CAPTAIN
Be you his eunuch, and your mute I'll be.
When my tongue blabs, then let mine eyes not see.

VIOLA
I thank thee. Lead me on.   *Exeunt*

Enter Sir Toby Belch and Maria   I.3

SIR TOBY What a plague means my niece to take the death
   of her brother thus? I am sure care's an enemy to life.

MARIA By my troth, Sir Toby, you must come in earlier
   o'nights. Your cousin, my lady, takes great exceptions to
   your ill hours.

SIR TOBY Why, let her except before excepted.

MARIA Ay, but you must confine yourself within the
   modest limits of order.

SIR TOBY Confine! I'll confine myself no finer than I am.
   These clothes are good enough to drink in, and so be   10
   these boots too; an they be not, let them hang themselves in their own straps.

MARIA That quaffing and drinking will undo you. I heard
   my lady talk of it yesterday, and of a foolish knight that

you brought in one night here, to be her wooer.

SIR TOBY Who? Sir Andrew Aguecheek?

MARIA Ay, he.

SIR TOBY He's as tall a man as any's in Illyria.

MARIA What's that to the purpose?

20   SIR TOBY Why, he has three thousand ducats a year.

MARIA Ay, but he'll have but a year in all these ducats.
He's a very fool and a prodigal.

SIR TOBY Fie, that you'll say so. He plays o'the viol-de-
gamboys, and speaks three or four languages word for
word without book, and hath all the good gifts of nature.

MARIA He hath indeed all, most natural; for besides that
he's a fool, he's a great quarreller; and but that he hath
the gift of a coward to allay the gust he hath in quarrel-
ling, 'tis thought among the prudent he would quickly
30   have the gift of a grave.

SIR TOBY By this hand, they are scoundrels and substractors that say so of him. Who are they?

MARIA They that add, moreover, he's drunk nightly in
your company.

SIR TOBY With drinking healths to my niece. I'll drink to
her as long as there is a passage in my throat and drink
in Illyria. He's a coward and a coistrel that will not
drink to my niece till his brains turn o'the toe, like a
parish top. What, wench! Castiliano, *vulgo* – for here
40   comes Sir Andrew Agueface!

Enter Sir Andrew Aguecheek

SIR ANDREW Sir Toby Belch! How now, Sir Toby
Belch?

SIR TOBY Sweet Sir Andrew!

SIR ANDREW Bless you, fair shrew.

MARIA And you too, sir.

SIR TOBY Accost, Sir Andrew, accost.

SIR ANDREW What's that?

SIR TOBY My niece's chambermaid.

SIR ANDREW Good Mistress Accost, I desire better acquaintance.   50

MARIA My name is Mary, sir.

SIR ANDREW Good Mistress Mary Accost —

SIR TOBY (*aside*) You mistake, knight. 'Accost' is front
her, board her, woo her, assail her.

SIR ANDREW (*aside*) By my troth, I would not undertake
her in this company. Is that the meaning of 'accost'?

MARIA Fare you well, gentlemen.

SIR TOBY (*aside*) An thou let part so, Sir Andrew, would
thou mightst never draw sword again.

SIR ANDREW An you part so, mistress, I would I might   60
never draw sword again. Fair lady, do you think you
have fools in hand?

MARIA Sir, I have not you by the hand.

SIR ANDREW Marry, but you shall have, and here's my
hand.

MARIA Now, sir, 'Thought is free.' I pray you, bring your
hand to the buttery bar and let it drink.

SIR ANDREW Wherefore, sweetheart? What's your metaphor?

MARIA It's dry, sir.   70

SIR ANDREW Why, I think so. I am not such an ass, but
I can keep my hand dry. But what's your jest?

MARIA A dry jest, sir.

SIR ANDREW Are you full of them?

MARIA Ay, sir. I have them at my fingers' ends. Marry,
now I let go your hand, I am barren.   *Exit*

SIR TOBY O knight, thou lack'st a cup of canary. When
did I see thee so put down?

SIR ANDREW Never in your life, I think, unless you see
canary put me down. Methinks sometimes I have no   80
more wit than a Christian or an ordinary man has; but I

am a great eater of beef, and I believe that does harm to
my wit.

SIR TOBY No question.

SIR ANDREW An I thought that, I'd forswear it. I'll ride
home tomorrow, Sir Toby.

SIR TOBY *Pourquoi*, my dear knight?

SIR ANDREW What is *pourquoi*? Do or not do? I would I
had bestowed that time in the tongues that I have in
90   fencing, dancing, and bear-baiting. O, had I but followed the arts!

SIR TOBY Then hadst thou had an excellent head of hair.

SIR ANDREW Why, would that have mended my hair?

SIR TOBY Past question, for thou seest it will not curl by
nature.

SIR ANDREW But it becomes me well enough, does't not?

SIR TOBY Excellent, it hangs like flax on a distaff; and I
hope to see a huswife take thee between her legs and
spin it off.

100   SIR ANDREW Faith, I'll home tomorrow, Sir Toby. Your
niece will not be seen, or if she be, it's four to one she'll
none of me; the Count himself, here hard by, woos her.

SIR TOBY She'll none o'the Count; she'll not match above
her degree, neither in estate, years, nor wit. I have heard
her swear't. Tut, there's life in't, man.

SIR ANDREW I'll stay a month longer. I am a fellow o'the
strangest mind i'the world. I delight in masques and
revels sometimes altogether.

SIR TOBY Art thou good at these kickshawses, knight?

110   SIR ANDREW As any man in Illyria, whatsoever he be,
under the degree of my betters, and yet I will not compare with an old man.

SIR TOBY What is thy excellence in a galliard, knight?

SIR ANDREW Faith, I can cut a caper.

SIR TOBY And I can cut the mutton to't.

SIR ANDREW And I think I have the back-trick, simply as
strong as any man in Illyria.

SIR TOBY Wherefore are these things hid? Wherefore
have these gifts a curtain before 'em? Are they like to
take dust, like Mistress Mall's picture? Why dost thou   120
not go to church in a galliard and come home in a
coranto? My very walk should be a jig. I would not so
much as make water but in a sink-apace. What dost thou
mean? Is it a world to hide virtues in? I did think by
the excellent constitution of thy leg it was formed under
the star of a galliard.

SIR ANDREW Ay, 'tis strong, and it does indifferent well
in a dun-coloured stock. Shall we set about some revels?

SIR TOBY What shall we do else? Were we not born under
Taurus?   130

SIR ANDREW Taurus? That's sides and heart.

SIR TOBY No, sir, it is legs and thighs. Let me see thee
caper. Ha! Higher! Ha! Ha! Excellent!   *Exeunt*

Enter Valentine, and Viola in man's attire   I.4

VALENTINE If the Duke continue these favours towards
you, Cesario, you are like to be much advanced. He hath
known you but three days, and already you are no
stranger.

VIOLA You either fear his humour or my negligence, that
you call in question the continuance of his love. Is he
inconstant, sir, in his favours?

VALENTINE No, believe me.

Enter Orsino, Curio, and attendants

VIOLA I thank you. Here comes the Count.

ORSINO Who saw Cesario, ho?   10

VIOLA On your attendance, my lord, here.

ORSINO (*to Curio and attendants*)
    Stand you awhile aloof. (*To Viola*) Cesario,
    Thou knowest no less but all. I have unclasped
    To thee the book even of my secret soul.
    Therefore, good youth, address thy gait unto her.
    Be not denied access; stand at her doors,
    And tell them, there thy fixèd foot shall grow
    Till thou have audience.
VIOLA   Sure, my noble lord,
    If she be so abandoned to her sorrow
20   As it is spoke, she never will admit me.
ORSINO
    Be clamorous and leap all civil bounds
    Rather than make unprofited return.
VIOLA
    Say I do speak with her, my lord, what then?
ORSINO
    O, then unfold the passion of my love.
    Surprise her with discourse of my dear faith.
    It shall become thee well to act my woes;
    She will attend it better in thy youth
    Than in a nuncio's of more grave aspect.
VIOLA
    I think not so, my lord.
ORSINO   Dear lad, believe it.
30   For they shall yet belie thy happy years
    That say thou art a man. Diana's lip
    Is not more smooth and rubious. Thy small pipe
    Is as the maiden's organ, shrill and sound,
    And all is semblative a woman's part.
    I know thy constellation is right apt
    For this affair. Some four or five attend him –
    All, if you will; for I myself am best
    When least in company. Prosper well in this,

And thou shalt live as freely as thy lord,
To call his fortunes thine.

VIOLA   I'll do my best   40
To woo your lady. (*Aside*) Yet, a barful strife!
Whoe'er I woo, myself would be his wife.   *Exeunt*

Enter Maria and Feste the Clown   I.5

MARIA Nay, either tell me where thou hast been, or I will
    not open my lips so wide as a bristle may enter, in way of
    thy excuse. My lady will hang thee for thy absence.

FESTE Let her hang me. He that is well hanged in this
    world needs to fear no colours.

MARIA Make that good.

FESTE He shall see none to fear.

MARIA A good lenten answer! I can tell thee where that
    saying was born, of 'I fear no colours.'

FESTE Where, good Mistress Mary?   10

MARIA In the wars; and that may you be bold to say in
    your foolery.

FESTE Well, God give them wisdom that have it; and
    those that are fools, let them use their talents.

MARIA Yet you will be hanged for being so long absent;
    or to be turned away – is not that as good as a hanging
    to you?

FESTE Many a good hanging prevents a bad marriage;
    and for turning away, let summer bear it out.

MARIA You are resolute, then?   20

FESTE Not so neither, but I am resolved on two points.

MARIA That if one break, the other will hold; or if both
    break, your gaskins fall.

FESTE Apt, in good faith, very apt. Well, go thy way, if
    Sir Toby would leave drinking, thou wert as witty a
    piece of Eve's flesh as any in Illyria.

MARIA Peace, you rogue, no more o'that. Here comes my
lady. Make your excuse wisely, you were best.   *Exit*
Enter Olivia with Malvolio and attendants

FESTE Wit, an't be thy will, put me into good fooling.
30   Those wits that think they have thee do very oft prove
fools; and I that am sure I lack thee may pass for a wise
man. For what says Quinapalus? 'Better a witty fool
than a foolish wit.' God bless thee, lady!

OLIVIA Take the fool away.

FESTE Do you not hear, fellows? Take away the lady.

OLIVIA Go to, y'are a dry fool. I'll no more of you. Besides, you grow dishonest.

FESTE Two faults, madonna, that drink and good counsel
will amend. For give the dry fool drink, then is the fool
40   not dry. Bid the dishonest man mend himself: if he
mend, he is no longer dishonest; if he cannot, let the
botcher mend him. Anything that's mended, is but
patched: virtue that transgresses is but patched with
sin; and sin that amends is but patched with virtue. If
that this simple syllogism will serve, so; if it will not,
what remedy? As there is no true cuckold but calamity,
so beauty's a flower. The lady bade take away the fool;
therefore I say again – take her away!

OLIVIA Sir, I bade them take away you.

50 FESTE Misprision in the highest degree! Lady, *cucullus
non facit monachum*; that's as much to say as I wear not
motley in my brain. Good madonna, give me leave to
prove you a fool.

OLIVIA Can you do it?

FESTE Dexteriously, good madonna.

OLIVIA Make your proof.

FESTE I must catechize you for it, madonna. Good my
mouse of virtue, answer me.

OLIVIA Well, sir, for want of other idleness, I'll bide your
60   proof.

FESTE Good madonna, why mourn'st thou?

OLIVIA Good fool, for my brother's death.

FESTE I think his soul is in hell, madonna.

OLIVIA I know his soul is in heaven, fool.

FESTE The more fool, madonna, to mourn for your
brother's soul, being in heaven. Take away the fool,
gentlemen.

OLIVIA What think you of this fool, Malvolio? Doth he
not mend?

MALVOLIO Yes, and shall do, till the pangs of death shake   70
him. Infirmity, that decays the wise, doth ever make the
better fool.

FESTE God send you, sir, a speedy infirmity for the better
increasing your folly. Sir Toby will be sworn that I am
no fox, but he will not pass his word for twopence that
you are no fool.

OLIVIA How say you to that, Malvolio?

MALVOLIO I marvel your ladyship takes delight in such a
barren rascal. I saw him put down the other day with an
ordinary fool that has no more brain than a stone. Look   80
you now, he's out of his guard already; unless you laugh
and minister occasion to him, he is gagged. I protest I
take these wise men, that crow so at these set kind of
fools, no better than the fools' zanies.

OLIVIA O, you are sick of self-love, Malvolio, and taste
with a distempered appetite. To be generous, guiltless,
and of free disposition, is to take those things for bird-
bolts that you deem cannon bullets. There is no slander
in an allowed fool, though he do nothing but rail; nor no
railing in a known discreet man, though he do nothing   90
but reprove.

FESTE Now Mercury endue thee with leasing, for thou
speak'st well of fools.

Enter Maria

MARIA Madam, there is at the gate a young gentleman
much desires to speak with you.

OLIVIA From the Count Orsino, is it?

MARIA I know not, madam. 'Tis a fair young man, and
well attended.

OLIVIA Who of my people hold him in delay?

100 MARIA Sir Toby, madam, your kinsman.

OLIVIA Fetch him off, I pray you, he speaks nothing but
madman. Fie on him! Go you, Malvolio. If it be a suit
from the Count, I am sick or not at home – what you
will, to dismiss it.   *Exit Malvolio*
Now you see, sir, how your fooling grows old and people
dislike it?

FESTE Thou hast spoke for us, madonna, as if thy eldest
son should be a fool; whose skull Jove cram with brains,
for – here he comes –
    (*Enter Sir Toby*)

110 one of thy kin has a most weak *pia mater*.

OLIVIA By mine honour, half drunk! What is he at the
gate, cousin?

SIR TOBY A gentleman.

OLIVIA A gentleman! What gentleman?

SIR TOBY 'Tis a gentleman here – a plague o'these pickle-
herring! (*To Feste*) How now, sot!

FESTE Good Sir Toby!

OLIVIA Cousin, cousin, how have you come so early by
this lethargy?

120 SIR TOBY Lechery! I defy lechery! There's one at the
gate.

OLIVIA Ay, marry, what is he?

SIR TOBY Let him be the devil an he will, I care not. Give
me faith, say I. Well, it's all one.
                    Exit Sir Toby, followed by Maria

OLIVIA What's a drunken man like, fool?

FESTE Like a drowned man, a fool, and a madman. One
    draught above heat makes him a fool, the second mads
    him, and a third drowns him.
OLIVIA Go thou and seek the crowner, and let him sit o'
    my coz, for he's in the third degree of drink – he's   130
    drowned. Go, look after him.
FESTE He is but mad yet, madonna, and the fool shall look
    to the madman.   *Exit*
    Enter Malvolio
MALVOLIO Madam, yond young fellow swears he will
    speak with you. I told him you were sick; he takes on
    him to understand so much, and therefore comes to
    speak with you. I told him you were asleep; he seems to
    have a foreknowledge of that too, and therefore comes
    to speak with you. What is to be said to him, lady? He's
    fortified against any denial.   140
OLIVIA Tell him, he shall not speak with me.
MALVOLIO He's been told so; and he says he'll stand at
    your door like a sheriff's post and be the supporter to a
    bench, but he'll speak with you.
OLIVIA What kind o'man is he?
MALVOLIO Why, of mankind.
OLIVIA What manner of man?
MALVOLIO Of very ill manner; he'll speak with you, will
    you or no.
OLIVIA Of what personage and years is he?   150
MALVOLIO Not yet old enough for a man, nor young
    enough for a boy; as a squash is before 'tis a peascod, or
    a codling when 'tis almost an apple. 'Tis with him in
    standing water between boy and man. He is very well-
    favoured, and he speaks very shrewishly. One would
    think his mother's milk were scarce out of him.
OLIVIA Let him approach. Call in my gentlewoman.
MALVOLIO Gentlewoman, my lady calls.   *Exit*

Enter Maria

OLIVIA
    Give me my veil. Come, throw it o'er my face.

160 We'll once more hear Orsino's embassy.

    Enter Viola

VIOLA The honourable lady of the house, which is she?

OLIVIA Speak to me, I shall answer for her. Your will?

VIOLA Most radiant, exquisite, and unmatchable beauty –
    I pray you, tell me if this be the lady of the house, for I
    never saw her. I would be loath to cast away my speech;
    for besides that it is excellently well penned, I have
    taken great pains to con it. Good beauties, let me sustain
    no scorn. I am very comptible, even to the least sinister
    usage.

170 OLIVIA Whence came you, sir?

VIOLA I can say little more than I have studied, and that
    question's out of my part. Good gentle one, give me
    modest assurance if you be the lady of the house, that I
    may proceed in my speech.

OLIVIA Are you a comedian?

VIOLA No, my profound heart; and yet, by the very fangs
    of malice, I swear I am not that I play. Are you the lady
    of the house?

OLIVIA If I do not usurp myself, I am.

180 VIOLA Most certain, if you are she, you do usurp your-
    self; for what is yours to bestow is not yours to reserve.
    But this is from my commission. I will on with my
    speech in your praise, and then show you the heart of
    my message.

OLIVIA Come to what is important in't. I forgive you the
    praise.

VIOLA Alas, I took great pains to study it, and 'tis poetical.

OLIVIA It is the more like to be feigned; I pray you, keep it
    in. I heard you were saucy at my gates, and allowed your

approach rather to wonder at you than to hear you. If   190
you be not mad, be gone; if you have reason, be brief.
'Tis not that time of moon with me, to make one in so
skipping a dialogue.

MARIA (*showing Viola the way out*) Will you hoist sail, sir?
Here lies your way.

VIOLA No, good swabber, I am to hull here a little longer.
Some mollification for your giant, sweet lady! Tell me
your mind; I am a messenger.

OLIVIA Sure, you have some hideous matter to deliver,
when the courtesy of it is so fearful. Speak your office.   200

VIOLA It alone concerns your ear. I bring no overture of
war, no taxation of homage. I hold the olive in my hand;
my words are as full of peace as matter.

OLIVIA Yet you began rudely. What are you? What
would you?

VIOLA The rudeness that hath appeared in me have I
learned from my entertainment. What I am and what I
would are as secret as maidenhead; to your ears divinity,
to any others profanation.

OLIVIA Give us the place alone.   210

                    Maria and attendants withdraw
We will hear this divinity. Now, sir, what is your text?

VIOLA Most sweet lady —

OLIVIA A comfortable doctrine, and much may be said of
it. Where lies your text?

VIOLA In Orsino's bosom.

OLIVIA In his bosom! In what chapter of his bosom?

VIOLA To answer by the method, in the first of his heart.

OLIVIA O, I have read it; it is heresy. Have you no more to
say?

VIOLA Good madam, let me see your face.   220

OLIVIA Have you any commission from your lord to ne-
gotiate with my face? You are now out of your text; but

we will draw the curtain and show you the picture. Look
you, sir, such a one I was this present. Is't not well
done?

VIOLA Excellently done – if God did all.

OLIVIA 'Tis in grain, sir, 'twill endure wind and weather.

VIOLA
'Tis beauty truly blent, whose red and white
Nature's own sweet and cunning hand laid on.
230 Lady, you are the cruellest she alive,
If you will lead these graces to the grave,
And leave the world no copy.

OLIVIA O, sir, I will not be so hard-hearted. I will give
out divers schedules of my beauty. It shall be inven-
toried, and every particle and utensil labelled to my will.
As, item: two lips, indifferent red; item: two grey eyes,
with lids to them; item: one neck, one chin, and so forth.
Were you sent hither to praise me?

VIOLA
I see you what you are, you are too proud.
240 But if you were the devil, you are fair.
My lord and master loves you – O, such love
Could be but recompensed, though you were crowned
The nonpareil of beauty!

OLIVIA   How does he love me?

VIOLA
With adorations, fertile tears,
With groans that thunder love, with sighs of fire.

OLIVIA
Your lord does know my mind, I cannot love him.
Yet I suppose him virtuous, know him noble,
Of great estate, of fresh and stainless youth,
In voices well divulged, free, learned, and valiant,
250 And in dimension and the shape of nature
A gracious person. But yet I cannot love him.

He might have took his answer long ago.

VIOLA

If I did love you in my master's flame,
With such a suffering, such a deadly life,
In your denial I would find no sense;
I would not understand it.

OLIVIA   Why, what would you?

VIOLA

Make me a willow cabin at your gate,
And call upon my soul within the house;
Write loyal cantons of contemnèd love
And sing them loud even in the dead of night;   260
Hallow your name to the reverberate hills
And make the babbling gossip of the air
Cry out 'Olivia!' O, you should not rest
Between the elements of air and earth,
But you should pity me.

OLIVIA   You might do much.
What is your parentage?

VIOLA

Above my fortunes, yet my state is well.
I am a gentleman.

OLIVIA   Get you to your lord.
I cannot love him. Let him send no more –
Unless, perchance, you come to me again   270
To tell me how he takes it. Fare you well.
I thank you for your pains. Spend this for me.

VIOLA

I am no fee'd post, lady; keep your purse.
My master, not myself, lacks recompense.
Love make his heart of flint, that you shall love,
And let your fervour like my master's be
Placed in contempt. Farewell, fair cruelty!   *Exit*

OLIVIA

    'What is your parentage?'
    'Above my fortunes, yet my state is well.

280   I am a gentleman.' I'll be sworn thou art.
    Thy tongue, thy face, thy limbs, actions, and spirit
    Do give thee fivefold blazon. Not too fast! soft, soft –
    Unless the master were the man. How now?
    Even so quickly may one catch the plague?
    Methinks I feel this youth's perfections,
    With an invisible and subtle stealth,
    To creep in at mine eyes. Well, let it be!
    What ho, Malvolio!

     Enter Malvolio

MALVOLIO

    Here, madam, at your service.

OLIVIA

290   Run after that same peevish messenger,
    The County's man. He left this ring behind him,
    Would I or not. Tell him, I'll none of it.
    Desire him not to flatter with his lord,
    Nor hold him up with hopes; I am not for him.
    If that the youth will come this way tomorrow,
    I'll give him reasons for't. Hie thee, Malvolio!

MALVOLIO

    Madam, I will.   *Exit*

OLIVIA

    I do I know not what, and fear to find
    Mine eye too great a flatterer for my mind.

300   Fate, show thy force; ourselves we do not owe.
    What is decreed must be, and be this so.   *Exit*

*

Enter Antonio and Sebastian

ANTONIO Will you stay no longer? Nor will you not that
    I go with you?

SEBASTIAN By your patience, no. My stars shine darkly
    over me. The malignancy of my fate might perhaps
    distemper yours; therefore I shall crave of you your
    leave, that I may bear my evils alone. It were a bad re-
    compense for your love to lay any of them on you.

ANTONIO Let me yet know of you whither you are bound.

SEBASTIAN No, sooth, sir; my determinate voyage is mere
    extravagancy. But I perceive in you so excellent a touch   10
    of modesty, that you will not extort from me what I am
    willing to keep in; therefore it charges me in manners
    the rather to express myself. You must know of me
    then, Antonio, my name is Sebastian which I called
    Roderigo. My father was that Sebastian of Messaline
    whom I know you have heard of. He left behind him
    myself and a sister, both born in an hour – if the
    heavens had been pleased, would we had so ended! But
    you, sir, altered that, for some hour before you took me
    from the breach of the sea was my sister drowned.   20

ANTONIO Alas the day!

SEBASTIAN A lady, sir, though it was said she much re-
    sembled me, was yet of many accounted beautiful. But
    though I could not with such estimable wonder over-far
    believe that, yet thus far I will boldly publish her: she
    bore a mind that envy could not but call fair. She is
    drowned already, sir, with salt water, though I seem to
    drown her remembrance again with more.

ANTONIO Pardon me, sir, your bad entertainment.

SEBASTIAN O good Antonio, forgive me your trouble.   30

ANTONIO If you will not murder me for my love, let me
    be your servant.

SEBASTIAN If you will not undo what you have done –

that is, kill him whom you have recovered – desire it not.
Fare ye well at once; my bosom is full of kindness, and I
am yet so near the manners of my mother that, upon the
least occasion more, mine eyes will tell tales of me. I am
bound to the Count Orsino's court. Farewell.   *Exit*

ANTONIO
    The gentleness of all the gods go with thee!
40   I have many enemies in Orsino's court,
    Else would I very shortly see thee there –
    But come what may, I do adore thee so
    That danger shall seem sport, and I will go!   *Exit*

II.2   *Enter Viola and Malvolio at several doors*

MALVOLIO Were not you even now with the Countess
    Olivia?

VIOLA Even now, sir; on a moderate pace I have since
    arrived but hither.

MALVOLIO She returns this ring to you, sir. You might
    have saved me my pains, to have taken it away yourself.
    She adds, moreover, that you should put your lord into
    a desperate assurance she will none of him; and one
    thing more, that you be never so hardy to come again in
10   his affairs – unless it be to report your lord's taking of
    this. Receive it so.

VIOLA She took the ring of me, I'll none of it.

MALVOLIO Come, sir, you peevishly threw it to her, and
    her will is it should be so returned. If it be worth stoop-
    ing for, there it lies in your eye; if not, be it his that finds
    it.   *Exit*

VIOLA
    I left no ring with her; what means this lady?
    Fortune forbid my outside have not charmed her!
    She made good view of me, indeed so much

That – methought – her eyes had lost her tongue,   20
For she did speak in starts, distractedly.
She loves me, sure, the cunning of her passion
Invites me in this churlish messenger.
None of my lord's ring? Why, he sent her none.
I am the man! If it be so – as 'tis –
Poor lady, she were better love a dream.
Disguise, I see thou art a wickedness
Wherein the pregnant enemy does much.
How easy is it for the proper false
In women's waxen hearts to set their forms.   30
Alas, our frailty is the cause, not we,
For such as we are made, if such we be.
How will this fadge? My master loves her dearly;
And I, poor monster, fond as much on him;
And she, mistaken, seems to dote on me.
What will become of this? As I am man,
My state is desperate for my master's love.
As I am woman – now, alas the day,
What thriftless sighs shall poor Olivia breathe!
O time, thou must untangle this, not I!   40
It is too hard a knot for me t'untie.   *Exit*

Enter Sir Toby and Sir Andrew   II.3

SIR TOBY Approach, Sir Andrew. Not to be abed after
    midnight, is to be up betimes, and *diluculo surgere*,
    thou knowest –
SIR ANDREW Nay, by my troth, I know not; but I know
    to be up late is to be up late.
SIR TOBY A false conclusion! I hate it as an unfilled can.
    To be up after midnight and to go to bed then is early;
    so that to go to bed after midnight is to go to bed be-
    times. Does not our lives consist of the four elements?

10 SIR ANDREW Faith, so they say; but I think it rather con-
sists of eating and drinking.

SIR TOBY Thou'rt a scholar. Let us therefore eat and
drink. Marian, I say! A stoup of wine!

Enter Feste

SIR ANDREW Here comes the fool, i'faith.

FESTE How now, my hearts! Did you never see the picture of We Three?

SIR TOBY Welcome, ass! Now let's have a catch.

SIR ANDREW By my troth, the fool has an excellent breast.
I had rather than forty shillings I had such a leg, and so
20 sweet a breath to sing, as the fool has. In sooth, thou
wast in very gracious fooling last night, when thou
spok'st of Pigrogromitus, of the Vapians passing the
equinoctial of Queubus. 'Twas very good, i'faith. I sent
thee sixpence for thy leman, hadst it?

FESTE I did impetticoat thy gratillity; for Malvolio's nose
is no whipstock, my lady has a white hand, and the
Myrmidons are no bottle-ale houses.

SIR ANDREW Excellent! Why, this is the best fooling,
when all is done. Now, a song!

30 SIR TOBY Come on, there is sixpence for you. Let's have a
song.

SIR ANDREW There's a testril of me, too. If one knight
give a —

FESTE Would you have a love song, or a song of good life?

SIR TOBY A love song! A love song!

SIR ANDREW Ay, ay, I care not for good life.

FESTE (*sings*)

O mistress mine! Where are you roaming?
O, stay and hear: your true love's coming,
That can sing both high and low.
40   Trip no further, pretty sweeting;

> Journeys end in lovers meeting,
>> Every wise man's son doth know.

SIR ANDREW Excellent good, i'faith.

SIR TOBY Good, good.

FESTE (*sings*)

> What is love? 'Tis not hereafter;
>> Present mirth hath present laughter,
>>> What's to come is still unsure.
> In delay there lies no plenty —
>> Then come kiss me, sweet and twenty,
>>> Youth's a stuff will not endure.   50

SIR ANDREW A mellifluous voice, as I am true knight.

SIR TOBY A contagious breath.

SIR ANDREW Very sweet and contagious, i'faith.

SIR TOBY To hear by the nose, it is dulcet in contagion. But shall we make the welkin dance indeed? Shall we rouse the night-owl in a catch that will draw three souls out of one weaver? Shall we do that?

SIR ANDREW An you love me, let's do't. I am dog at a catch.

FESTE By'r lady, sir, and some dogs will catch well.   60

SIR ANDREW Most certain. Let our catch be 'Thou knave'.

FESTE 'Hold thy peace, thou knave', knight? I shall be constrained in't to call thee knave, knight.

SIR ANDREW 'Tis not the first time I have constrained one to call me knave. Begin, fool; it begins (*he sings*)
> Hold thy peace —

FESTE I shall never begin if I hold my peace.

SIR ANDREW Good, i'faith. Come, begin!

Catch sung. Enter Maria

MARIA What a caterwauling do you keep here! If my lady   70
have not called up her steward Malvolio and bid him
turn you out of doors, never trust me.

SIR TOBY My lady's a — Cataian; we are — politicians;
Malvolio's a — Peg-a-Ramsey; and (*he sings*)
       Three merry men be we!
Am not I consanguineous? Am I not of her blood?
Tilly-vally! 'Lady'! (*He sings*)
       There dwelt a man in Babylon, lady, lady —
FESTE Beshrew me, the knight's in admirable fooling.
80 SIR ANDREW Ay, he does well enough if he be disposed,
and so do I too. He does it with a better grace, but I do
it more natural.
SIR TOBY (*sings*)
       O' the twelfth day of December —
MARIA For the love o'God, peace!
Enter Malvolio
MALVOLIO My masters, are you mad? Or what are you?
Have you no wit, manners, nor honesty, but to gabble
like tinkers at this time of night? Do ye make an alehouse of my lady's house, that ye squeak out your
coziers' catches without any mitigation or remorse of
90 voice? Is there no respect of place, persons, nor time in
you?
SIR TOBY We did keep time, sir, in our catches. Sneck up!
MALVOLIO Sir Toby, I must be round with you. My lady
bade me tell you that, though she harbours you as her
kinsman, she's nothing allied to your disorders. If you
can separate yourself and your misdemeanours, you are
welcome to the house. If not, an it would please you to
take leave of her, she is very willing to bid you farewell.
SIR TOBY (*sings*)
       Farewell, dear heart, since I must needs be gone —
100 MARIA Nay, good Sir Toby!
FESTE (*sings*)
       His eyes do show his days are almost done —
MALVOLIO Is't even so!

SIR TOBY (*sings*)
              But I will never die –
FESTE (*sings*)
              Sir Toby, there you lie –
MALVOLIO This is much credit to you!
SIR TOBY (*sings*)
              Shall I bid him go?
FESTE (*sings*)
              What an if you do?
SIR TOBY (*sings*)
              Shall I bid him go and spare not?
FESTE (*sings*)
              O no, no, no, no, you dare not!
SIR TOBY Out o'tune, sir, ye lie. (*To Malvolio*) Art any   110
    more than a steward? Dost thou think, because thou art
    virtuous, there shall be no more cakes and ale?
FESTE Yes, by Saint Anne, and ginger shall be hot i'the
    mouth, too.
SIR TOBY Th'art i'the right. (*To Malvolio*) Go, sir, rub
    your chain with crumbs. A stoup of wine, Maria!
MALVOLIO Mistress Mary, if you prized my lady's favour
    at anything more than contempt, you would not give
    means for this uncivil rule. She shall know of it, by this
    hand!   *Exit*   120
MARIA Go, shake your ears.
SIR ANDREW 'Twere as good a deed as to drink when a
    man's a-hungry, to challenge him the field and then to
    break promise with him and make a fool of him.
SIR TOBY Do't, knight, I'll write thee a challenge; or I'll
    deliver thy indignation to him by word of mouth.
MARIA Sweet Sir Toby, be patient for tonight. Since the
    youth of the Count's was today with my lady, she is
    much out of quiet. For Monsieur Malvolio, let me alone
    with him. If I do not gull him into a nayword, and make   130

him a common recreation, do not think I have wit
enough to lie straight in my bed. I know I can do it.

SIR TOBY Possess us, possess us, tell us something of him.

MARIA Marry, sir, sometimes he is a kind of puritan —

SIR ANDREW O, if I thought that, I'd beat him like a dog.

SIR TOBY What, for being a puritan? Thy exquisite reason, dear knight?

SIR ANDREW I have no exquisite reason for't, but I have
reason good enough.

140 MARIA The devil a puritan that he is, or anything, con-
stantly, but a time-pleaser, an affectioned ass that cons
state without book and utters it by great swathes; the
best persuaded of himself, so crammed, as he thinks,
with excellencies, that it is his grounds of faith that all
that look on him love him — and on that vice in him will
my revenge find notable cause to work.

SIR TOBY What wilt thou do?

MARIA I will drop in his way some obscure epistles of
love; wherein, by the colour of his beard, the shape of
150 his leg, the manner of his gait, the expressure of his eye,
forehead, and complexion, he shall find himself most
feelingly personated. I can write very like my lady, your
niece; on a forgotten matter we can hardly make distinction of our hands.

SIR TOBY Excellent! I smell a device.

SIR ANDREW I have't in my nose too.

SIR TOBY He shall think by the letters that thou wilt
drop that they come from my niece, and that she's in
love with him.

160 MARIA My purpose is indeed a horse of that colour.

SIR ANDREW And your horse now would make him an
ass.

MARIA Ass, I doubt not.

SIR ANDREW O, 'twill be admirable!

MARIA Sport royal, I warrant you. I know my physic will
    work with him. I will plant you two, and let the fool
    make a third, where he shall find the letter. Observe his
    construction of it. For this night, to bed, and dream on
    the event. Farewell.   *Exit*
SIR TOBY Good night, Penthesilea.   170
SIR ANDREW Before me, she's a good wench.
SIR TOBY She's a beagle true bred, and one that adores
    me – what o'that?
SIR ANDREW I was adored once, too.
SIR TOBY Let's to bed, knight. Thou hadst need send for
    more money.
SIR ANDREW If I cannot recover your niece, I am a foul
    way out.
SIR TOBY Send for money, knight. If thou hast her not
    i'the end, call me cut.   180
SIR ANDREW If I do not, never trust me, take it how you
    will.
SIR TOBY Come, come, I'll go burn some sack, 'tis too
    late to go to bed now. Come, knight; come, knight.
                                                Exeunt

Enter Orsino, Viola, Curio, and others   II.4
ORSINO
    Give me some music! Now, good morrow, friends!
    Now, good Cesario, but that piece of song,
    That old and antique song we heard last night.
    Methought it did relieve my passion much,
    More than light airs and recollected terms
    Of these most brisk and giddy-pacèd times.
    Come, but one verse.
CURIO He is not here, so please your lordship, that should
    sing it.

10 ORSINO Who was it?

CURIO Feste the jester, my lord, a fool that the Lady
   Olivia's father took much delight in. He is about the
   house.

ORSINO Seek him out, and play the tune the while.

                                        Exit Curio

     Music plays
     Come hither, boy. If ever thou shalt love,
     In the sweet pangs of it, remember me.
     For such as I am, all true lovers are:
     Unstaid and skittish in all motions else,
     Save in the constant image of the creature
20   That is beloved. How dost thou like this tune?

VIOLA
     It gives a very echo to the seat
     Where love is throned.

ORSINO   Thou dost speak masterly.
     My life upon't, young though thou art, thine eye
     Hath stayed upon some favour that it loves.
     Hath it not, boy?

VIOLA   A little, by your favour.

ORSINO
     What kind of woman is't?

VIOLA   Of your complexion.

ORSINO
     She is not worth thee, then. What years, i'faith?

VIOLA
     About your years, my lord.

ORSINO
     Too old, by heaven. Let still the woman take
30   An elder than herself; so wears she to him;
     So sways she level in her husband's heart.
     For, boy, however we do praise ourselves,
     Our fancies are more giddy and unfirm,

More longing, wavering, sooner lost and worn,
Than women's are.

VIOLA　　　　　　　I think it well, my lord.

ORSINO

Then let thy love be younger than thyself,
Or thy affection cannot hold the bent.
For women are as roses whose fair flower,
Being once displayed, doth fall that very hour.

VIOLA

And so they are. Alas, that they are so,　　　　　　40
To die, even when they to perfection grow.

Enter Curio and Feste

ORSINO

O, fellow, come, the song we had last night.
Mark it, Cesario; it is old and plain.
The spinsters, and the knitters in the sun,
And the free maids that weave their thread with bones,
Do use to chant it. It is silly sooth,
And dallies with the innocence of love
Like the old age.

FESTE

Are you ready, sir?

ORSINO　　　　　　Ay, prithee sing.

Music plays

FESTE (*sings*)

Come away, come away, death,　　　　　　　　　50
　　And in sad cypress let me be laid.
Fie away, fie away, breath!
　　I am slain by a fair cruel maid.
My shroud of white, stuck all with yew,
　　O, prepare it!
My part of death, no one so true
　　Did share it.

Not a flower, not a flower sweet
   On my black coffin let there be strewn.
60 Not a friend, not a friend greet
   My poor corpse, where my bones shall be thrown.
A thousand thousand sighs to save,
     Lay me, O, where
Sad true lover never find my grave
     To weep there.

ORSINO There's for thy pains.

He gives Feste money

FESTE No pains, sir. I take pleasure in singing, sir.

ORSINO I'll pay thy pleasure, then.

FESTE Truly, sir, and pleasure will be paid, one time or
70 another.

ORSINO Give me now leave, to leave thee.

FESTE Now the melancholy god protect thee, and the
tailor make thy doublet of changeable taffeta, for thy
mind is a very opal. I would have men of such constancy put to sea, that their business might be everything, and their intent everywhere; for that's it that
always makes a good voyage of nothing. Farewell.

Exit Feste

ORSINO
   Let all the rest give place.

Curio and attendants withdraw
                  Once more, Cesario,
Get thee to yond same sovereign cruelty.
80 Tell her my love, more noble than the world,
Prizes not quantity of dirty lands.
The parts that fortune hath bestowed upon her
Tell her I hold as giddily as fortune.
But 'tis that miracle and queen of gems
That nature pranks her in, attracts my soul.

VIOLA

But if she cannot love you, sir?

ORSINO

It cannot be so answered.

VIOLA   Sooth, but you must.

Say that some lady, as perhaps there is,

Hath for your love as great a pang of heart

As you have for Olivia. You cannot love her.   90

You tell her so. Must she not then be answered?

ORSINO

There is no woman's sides

Can bide the beating of so strong a passion

As love doth give my heart; no woman's heart

So big to hold so much, they lack retention.

Alas, their love may be called appetite,

No motion of the liver, but the palate,

That suffer surfeit, cloyment, and revolt.

But mine is all as hungry as the sea,

And can digest as much. Make no compare   100

Between that love a woman can bear me

And that I owe Olivia.

VIOLA   Ay, but I know —

ORSINO

What dost thou know?

VIOLA

Too well what love women to men may owe.

In faith, they are as true of heart as we.

My father had a daughter loved a man —

As it might be perhaps, were I a woman,

I should your lordship.

ORSINO   And what's her history?

VIOLA

A blank, my lord. She never told her love,

But let concealment, like a worm i'the bud,   110

Feed on her damask cheek. She pined in thought,
And with a green and yellow melancholy,
She sat like Patience on a monument,
Smiling at grief. Was not this love indeed?
We men may say more, swear more, but indeed
Our shows are more than will; for still we prove
Much in our vows, but little in our love.

ORSINO
But died thy sister of her love, my boy?

VIOLA
I am all the daughters of my father's house,
120   And all the brothers too; and yet, I know not . . .
Sir, shall I to this lady?

ORSINO   Ay, that's the theme.
To her in haste; give her this jewel; say
My love can give no place, bide no denay.   *Exeunt*

II.5   *Enter Sir Toby, Sir Andrew, and Fabian*
SIR TOBY Come thy ways, Signor Fabian.
FABIAN Nay, I'll come. If I lose a scruple of this sport,
    let me be boiled to death with melancholy.
SIR TOBY Wouldst thou not be glad to have the nig-
    gardly, rascally sheep-biter come by some notable
    shame?
FABIAN I would exult, man. You know he brought me
    out o'favour with my lady about a bear-baiting here.
SIR TOBY To anger him, we'll have the bear again, and
10 we will fool him black and blue – shall we not, Sir
    Andrew?
SIR ANDREW An we do not, it is pity of our lives.
    Enter Maria
SIR TOBY Here comes the little villain. How now, my
    metal of India?

MARIA Get ye all three into the box-tree. Malvolio's
coming down this walk, he has been yonder i'the sun
practising behaviour to his own shadow this half-hour.
Observe him, for the love of mockery, for I know this
letter will make a contemplative idiot of him. Close, in
the name of jesting!   20
    The men hide. Maria throws down a letter
Lie thou there – for here comes the trout that must be
caught with tickling.   *Exit*
    Enter Malvolio
MALVOLIO 'Tis but fortune, all is fortune. Maria once
told me she did affect me; and I have heard herself
come thus near, that should she fancy, it should be one
of my complexion. Besides, she uses me with a more
exalted respect than anyone else that follows her. What
should I think on't?
SIR TOBY Here's an overweening rogue!
FABIAN O, peace! Contemplation makes a rare turkey-   30
cock of him; how he jets under his advanced plumes!
SIR ANDREW 'Slight, I could so beat the rogue!
SIR TOBY Peace, I say!
MALVOLIO To be Count Malvolio . . .
SIR TOBY Ah, rogue!
SIR ANDREW Pistol him, pistol him!
SIR TOBY Peace, peace!
MALVOLIO There is example for't. The lady of the
Strachy married the yeoman of the wardrobe.
SIR ANDREW Fie on him! Jezebel!   40
FABIAN O, peace! Now he's deeply in. Look how
imagination blows him.
MALVOLIO Having been three months married to her,
sitting in my state . . .
SIR TOBY O for a stone-bow to hit him in the eye!
MALVOLIO Calling my officers about me, in my branched

velvet gown, having come from a day-bed, where I have
left Olivia sleeping ...

SIR TOBY Fire and brimstone!

50 FABIAN O, peace, peace!

MALVOLIO And then to have the humour of state; and
after a demure travel of regard – telling them I know my
place, as I would they should do theirs – to ask for my
kinsman Toby.

SIR TOBY Bolts and shackles!

FABIAN O, peace, peace, peace! Now, now!

MALVOLIO Seven of my people, with an obedient start,
make out for him. I frown the while, and perchance
wind up my watch, or play with my (*fingering his*
60 *steward's chain of office*) – some rich jewel. Toby
approaches, curtsies there to me ...

SIR TOBY Shall this fellow live?

FABIAN Though our silence be drawn from us with cars,
yet peace!

MALVOLIO I extend my hand to him thus – quenching
my familiar smile with an austere regard of control ...

SIR TOBY And does not Toby take you a blow o'the lips
then?

MALVOLIO Saying, Cousin Toby, my fortunes having
70 cast me on your niece give me this prerogative of
speech ...

SIR TOBY What, what!

MALVOLIO You must amend your drunkenness.

SIR TOBY Out, scab!

FABIAN Nay, patience, or we break the sinews of our plot.

MALVOLIO Besides, you waste the treasure of your time
with a foolish knight ...

SIR ANDREW That's me, I warrant you.

MALVOLIO One Sir Andrew.

80 SIR ANDREW I knew 'twas I, for many do call me fool.

MALVOLIO (*picks up the letter*) What employment have we here?

FABIAN Now is the woodcock near the gin.

SIR TOBY O, peace, and the spirit of humours intimate reading aloud to him!

MALVOLIO By my life, this is my lady's hand. These be her very C's, her U's and her T's; and thus makes she her great P's. It is, in contempt of question, her hand.

SIR ANDREW Her C's, her U's and her T's? Why that?

MALVOLIO (*reads*)

To the unknown beloved this, and my good wishes.   90

Her very phrases! By your leave, wax. Soft! and the impressure her Lucrece, with which she uses to seal. 'Tis my lady! To whom should this be?

FABIAN This wins him, liver and all.

MALVOLIO (*reads*)

Jove knows I love;
    But who?
Lips, do not move;
    No man must know.

'No man must know'! What follows? The numbers altered! 'No man must know'! If this should be thee,   100 Malvolio!

SIR TOBY Marry, hang thee, brock!

MALVOLIO (*reads*)

I may command where I adore;
    But silence, like a Lucrece' knife,
With bloodless stroke my heart doth gore;
    M.O.A.I. doth sway my life.

FABIAN A fustian riddle!

SIR TOBY Excellent wench, say I!

MALVOLIO 'M.O.A.I. doth sway my life.' Nay, but first let me see, let me see, let me see . . .   110

FABIAN What dish o'poison has she dressed him!

SIR TOBY And with what wing the staniel checks at it!

MALVOLIO 'I may command where I adore.' Why, she may command me. I serve her, she is my lady. Why, this is evident to any formal capacity. There is no obstruction in this. And the end: what should that alphabetical position portend? If I could make that resemble something in me ... Softly, 'M.O.A.I.' ...

SIR TOBY O, ay, make up that. He is now at a cold scent.

120 FABIAN Sowter will cry upon't for all this, though it be as rank as a fox.

MALVOLIO M ... Malvolio! M! Why, that begins my name!

FABIAN Did not I say he would work it out? The cur is excellent at faults.

MALVOLIO M! But then there is no consonancy in the sequel that suffers under probation. A should follow, but O does.

FABIAN And O shall end, I hope.

130 SIR TOBY Ay, or I'll cudgel him and make him cry O.

MALVOLIO And then I comes behind.

FABIAN Ay, an you had any eye behind you, you might see more detraction at your heels than fortunes before you.

MALVOLIO M.O.A.I. This simulation is not as the former. And yet, to crush this a little, it would bow to me, for every one of these letters are in my name. Soft! Here follows prose.

He reads

If this fall into thy hand, revolve. In my stars I am above
140 *thee, but be not afraid of greatness. Some are born great,*
some achieve greatness, and some have greatness thrust
upon 'em. Thy fates open their hands, let thy blood and
spirit embrace them; and to inure thyself to what thou art

like to be, cast thy humble slough and appear fresh. Be
opposite with a kinsman, surly with servants. Let thy
tongue tang arguments of state. Put thyself into the trick of
singularity. She thus advises thee that sighs for thee.
Remember who commended thy yellow stockings and wished
to see thee ever cross-gartered. I say, remember. Go to, thou
art made if thou desirest to be so. If not, let me see thee a   150
steward still, the fellow of servants, and not worthy to
touch Fortune's fingers. Farewell. She that would alter
services with thee, The Fortunate Unhappy.

Daylight and champain discovers not more! This is
open. I will be proud, I will read politic authors, I will
baffle Sir Toby, I will wash off gross acquaintance, I
will be point-devise the very man. I do not now fool
myself, to let imagination jade me; for every reason
excites to this, that my lady loves me. She did commend
my yellow stockings of late, she did praise my leg being   160
cross-gartered; and in this she manifests herself to my
love and with a kind of injunction drives me to these
habits of her liking. I thank my stars, I am happy! I
will be strange, stout, in yellow stockings and cross-
gartered, even with the swiftness of putting on. Jove and
my stars be praised! Here is yet a postcript.

He reads

Thou canst not choose but know who I am. If thou enter-
tainest my love, let it appear in thy smiling, thy smiles
become thee well. Therefore in my presence still smile, dear
my sweet, I prithee.   170

Jove, I thank thee! I will smile. I will do everything that
thou wilt have me!   *Exit*
FABIAN I will not give my part of this sport for a pension
of thousands to be paid from the Sophy.

SIR TOBY I could marry this wench for this device.

SIR ANDREW So could I too.

SIR TOBY And ask no other dowry with her but such another jest.

SIR ANDREW Nor I neither.

Enter Maria

180 FABIAN Here comes my noble gull-catcher.

SIR TOBY Wilt thou set thy foot o' my neck?

SIR ANDREW Or o' mine either?

SIR TOBY Shall I play my freedom at tray-trip and become thy bondslave?

SIR ANDREW I'faith, or I either?

SIR TOBY Why, thou hast put him in such a dream, that
when the image of it leaves him, he must run mad.

MARIA Nay, but say true: does it work upon him?

SIR TOBY Like aqua-vitae with a midwife.

190 MARIA If you will then see the fruits of the sport, mark
his first approach before my lady. He will come to her in
yellow stockings, and 'tis a colour she abhors; and cross-
gartered, a fashion she detests; and he will smile upon
her, which will now be so unsuitable to her disposition –
being addicted to a melancholy as she is – that it cannot
but turn him into a notable contempt. If you will see it,
follow me.

SIR TOBY To the gates of Tartar, thou most excellent
devil of wit!

200 SIR ANDREW I'll make one too.   *Exeunt*

*

Enter at different entrances Viola, and Feste playing   III.I
  his pipe and tabor

VIOLA Save thee, friend, and thy music. Dost thou live by
  thy tabor?

FESTE No, sir, I live by the church.

VIOLA Art thou a Churchman?

FESTE No such matter, sir; I do live by the church. For I
  do live at my house, and my house doth stand by the
  church.

VIOLA So thou mayst say the king lies by a beggar, if a
  beggar dwell near him; or the Church stands by thy
  tabor, if thy tabor stand by the church.   10

FESTE You have said, sir. To see this age! A sentence is
  but a cheveril glove to a good wit; how quickly the
  wrong side may be turned outward!

VIOLA Nay, that's certain. They that dally nicely with
  words may quickly make them wanton.

FESTE I would therefore my sister had had no name, sir.

VIOLA Why, man?

FESTE Why, sir, her name's a word, and to dally with that
  word might make my sister wanton. But indeed, words
  are very rascals, since bonds disgraced them.   20

VIOLA Thy reason, man?

FESTE Troth, sir, I can yield you none without words, and
  words are grown so false, I am loath to prove reason
  with them.

VIOLA I warrant thou art a merry fellow, and car'st for
  nothing.

FESTE Not so, sir. I do care for something; but in my con-
  science, sir, I do not care for you. If that be to care for
  nothing, sir, I would it would make you invisible.

VIOLA Art not thou the Lady Olivia's fool?   30

FESTE No indeed, sir, the Lady Olivia has no folly. She
  will keep no fool, sir, till she be married, and fools are as

like husbands as pilchers are to herrings; the husband's
the bigger. I am indeed not her fool, but her corrupter
of words.

VIOLA I saw thee late at the Count Orsino's.

FESTE Foolery, sir, does walk about the orb like the sun, it
shines everywhere. I would be sorry, sir, but the fool
should be as oft with your master as with my mistress.
I think I saw your wisdom there?

VIOLA Nay, an thou pass upon me, I'll no more with
thee. Hold, there's expenses for thee!

She gives him a coin

FESTE Now Jove, in his next commodity of hair, send
thee a beard!

VIOLA By my troth, I'll tell thee, I am almost sick for
one – (*aside*) though I would not have it grow on my
chin. Is thy lady within?

FESTE Would not a pair of these have bred, sir?

VIOLA Yes, being kept together and put to use.

FESTE I would play Lord Pandarus of Phrygia, sir, to
bring a Cressida to this Troilus.

VIOLA I understand you, sir; 'tis well begged.

She gives another coin

FESTE The matter, I hope, is not great, sir, begging but a
beggar – Cressida was a beggar. My lady is within, sir.
I will conster to them whence you come. Who you are
and what you would are out of my welkin – I might say
'element', but the word is overworn.   *Exit*

VIOLA

This fellow is wise enough to play the fool;
And to do that well craves a kind of wit.
He must observe their mood on whom he jests,
The quality of persons, and the time,
And, like the haggard, check at every feather
That comes before his eye. This is a practice

As full of labour as a wise man's art.
For folly that he wisely shows is fit;
But wise men, folly-fallen, quite taint their wit.
Enter Sir Toby and Sir Andrew

SIR TOBY Save you, gentleman!

VIOLA And you, sir!

SIR ANDREW *Dieu vous garde, monsieur!*

VIOLA *Et vous aussi; votre serviteur!*   70

SIR ANDREW I hope, sir, you are, and I am yours.

SIR TOBY Will you encounter the house? My niece is
desirous you should enter, if your trade be to her.

VIOLA I am bound to your niece, sir. I mean, she is the
list of my voyage.

SIR TOBY Taste your legs, sir; put them to motion.

VIOLA My legs do better under-stand me, sir, than I
understand what you mean by bidding me taste my legs.

SIR TOBY I mean to go, sir, to enter.

VIOLA I will answer you with gate and entrance.   80
Enter Olivia and Maria
But we are prevented. (*To Olivia*) Most excellent,
accomplished lady, the heavens rain odours on you!

SIR ANDREW (*aside*) That youth's a rare courtier. 'Rain
odours'! Well!

VIOLA My matter hath no voice, lady, but to your own
most pregnant and vouchsafed ear.

SIR ANDREW 'Odours'; 'pregnant'; and 'vouchsafed'.
I'll get 'em all three all ready.

OLIVIA Let the garden door be shut and leave me to my
hearing.   90
Exeunt Sir Toby and Maria,
Sir Andrew lingering before he, too, leaves
Give me your hand, sir.

VIOLA
My duty, madam, and most humble service!

OLIVIA

    What is your name?

VIOLA

    Cesario is your servant's name, fair princess.

OLIVIA

    My servant, sir? 'Twas never merry world

    Since lowly feigning was called compliment.

    Y'are servant to the Count Orsino, youth.

VIOLA

    And he is yours, and his must needs be yours.

    Your servant's servant is your servant, madam.

OLIVIA

100   For him, I think not on him. For his thoughts,

    Would they were blanks rather than filled with me.

VIOLA

    Madam, I come to whet your gentle thoughts

    On his behalf —

OLIVIA   O, by your leave, I pray you.

    I bade you never speak again of him.

    But would you undertake another suit,

    I had rather hear you to solicit that

    Than music from the spheres.

VIOLA   Dear lady —

OLIVIA

    Give me leave, beseech you. I did send,

    After the last enchantment you did here,

110   A ring in chase of you. So did I abuse

    Myself, my servant, and, I fear me, you.

    Under your hard construction must I sit,

    To force that on you in a shameful cunning

    Which you knew none of yours. What might you think?

    Have you not set mine honour at the stake,

    And baited it with all th'unmuzzled thoughts

    That tyrannous heart can think? To one of your

        receiving

Enough is shown; a cypress, not a bosom,
Hides my heart. So let me hear you speak.

VIOLA

I pity you.

OLIVIA   That's a degree to love.   120

VIOLA

No, not a grize; for 'tis a vulgar proof
That very oft we pity enemies.

OLIVIA

Why, then, methinks 'tis time to smile again.
O world, how apt the poor are to be proud!
If one should be a prey, how much the better
To fall before the lion than the wolf!

    Clock strikes

The clock upbraids me with the waste of time.
Be not afraid, good youth; I will not have you.
And yet, when wit and youth is come to harvest,
Your wife is like to reap a proper man.   130
There lies your way, due west.

VIOLA   Then westward ho!
Grace and good disposition attend your ladyship.
You'll nothing, madam, to my lord by me?

OLIVIA

Stay.
I prithee, tell me what thou think'st of me?

VIOLA

That you do think you are not what you are.

OLIVIA

If I think so, I think the same of you.

VIOLA

Then think you right; I am not what I am.

OLIVIA

I would you were as I would have you be.

VIOLA
140   Would it be better, madam, than I am?
       I wish it might, for now I am your fool.
OLIVIA (*aside*)
       O, what a deal of scorn looks beautiful
       In the contempt and anger of his lip!
       A murderous guilt shows not itself more soon
       Than love that would seem hid; love's night is noon.
       (*To Viola*) Cesario, by the roses of the spring,
       By maidhood, honour, truth, and everything,
       I love thee so that, maugre all thy pride,
       Nor wit nor reason can my passion hide.
       Do not extort thy reasons from this clause:
150   For that I woo, thou therefore hast no cause.
       But rather reason thus with reason fetter:
       Love sought, is good; but given unsought, is better.
VIOLA
       By innocence I swear, and by my youth,
       I have one heart, one bosom, and one truth.
       And that no woman has, nor never none
       Shall mistress be of it, save I alone.
       And so, adieu, good madam; never more
       Will I my master's tears to you deplore.
OLIVIA
160   Yet come again; for thou perhaps mayst move
       That heart, which now abhors, to like his love.

                                             Exeunt

III.2   *Enter Sir Toby, Sir Andrew, and Fabian*
       SIR ANDREW No, faith, I'll not stay a jot longer.
       SIR TOBY Thy reason, dear venom, give thy reason.
       FABIAN You must needs yield your reason, Sir Andrew.
       SIR ANDREW Marry, I saw your niece do more favours to

the Count's servingman than ever she bestowed upon
me. I saw't i'the orchard.

SIR TOBY Did she see thee the while, old boy, tell me
that?

SIR ANDREW As plain as I see you now.

FABIAN This was a great argument of love in her toward   10
you.

SIR ANDREW 'Slight! Will you make an ass o'me?

FABIAN I will prove it legitimate, sir, upon the oaths of
judgement and reason.

SIR TOBY And they have been grand-jury men since before Noah was a sailor.

FABIAN She did show favour to the youth in your sight
only to exasperate you, to awake your dormouse valour,
to put fire in your heart and brimstone in your liver. You
should then have accosted her, and with some excellent   20
jests fire-new from the mint, you should have banged
the youth into dumbness. This was looked for at your
hand, and this was baulked. The double gilt of this
opportunity you let time wash off, and you are now
sailed into the north of my lady's opinion; where you
will hang like an icicle on a Dutchman's beard, unless you
do redeem it by some laudable attempt either of valour
or policy.

SIR ANDREW An't be any way, it must be with valour, for
policy I hate. I had as lief be a Brownist as a politician.   30

SIR TOBY Why then, build me thy fortunes upon the basis
of valour. Challenge me the Count's youth to fight with
him; hurt him in eleven places; my niece shall take note
of it — and, assure thyself, there is no love-broker in the
world can more prevail in man's commendation with
woman than report of valour.

FABIAN There is no way but this, Sir Andrew.

SIR ANDREW Will either of you bear me a challenge to
him?

40 SIR TOBY Go, write it in a martial hand. Be curst and
   brief. It is no matter how witty, so it be eloquent and
   full of invention. Taunt him with the licence of ink. If
   thou 'thou'-est him some thrice it shall not be amiss, and
   as many lies as will lie in thy sheet of paper – although
   the sheet were big enough for the bed of Ware in England, set 'em down, go about it. Let there be gall enough
   in thy ink, though thou write with a goose pen, no
   matter. About it!

SIR ANDREW Where shall I find you?

50 SIR TOBY We'll call thee at thy cubiculo. Go!

Exit Sir Andrew

FABIAN This is a dear manikin to you, Sir Toby.

SIR TOBY I have been dear to him, lad, some two thousand strong or so.

FABIAN We shall have a rare letter from him. But you'll
   not deliver it?

SIR TOBY Never trust me then – and by all means stir on
   the youth to an answer. I think oxen and wain-ropes
   cannot hale them together. For Andrew, if he were
   opened and you find so much blood in his liver as will

60 clog the foot of a flea, I'll eat the rest of the anatomy.

FABIAN And his opposite the youth bears in his visage no
   great presage of cruelty.

Enter Maria

SIR TOBY Look where the youngest wren of nine comes.

MARIA If you desire the spleen, and will laugh yourselves
   into stitches, follow me. Yond gull Malvolio is turned
   heathen, a very renegado; for there is no Christian, that
   means to be saved by believing rightly, can ever believe
   such impossible passages of grossness. He's in yellow
   stockings!

70 SIR TOBY And cross-gartered?

MARIA Most villainously; like a pedant that keeps a

school i'the church. I have dogged him like his mur-
derer. He does obey every point of the letter that I
dropped to betray him. He does smile his face into more
lines than is in the new map with the augmentation of
the Indies. You have not seen such a thing as 'tis. I can
hardly forbear hurling things at him; I know my lady
will strike him. If she do, he'll smile, and take if for a
great favour.

SIR TOBY Come, bring us, bring us where he is. *Exeunt* 80

Enter Sebastian and Antonio   III.3

SEBASTIAN
    I would not by my will have troubled you.
    But since you make your pleasure of your pains,
    I will no further chide you.

ANTONIO
    I could not stay behind you. My desire,
    More sharp than filèd steel, did spur me forth,
    And not all love to see you – though so much
    As might have drawn one to a longer voyage –
    But jealousy what might befall your travel,
    Being skill-less in these parts; which to a stranger,
    Unguided and unfriended, often prove   10
    Rough and unhospitable. My willing love,
    The rather by these arguments of fear,
    Set forth in your pursuit.

SEBASTIAN   My kind Antonio,
    I can no other answer make but thanks,
    And thanks. And ever oft good turns
    Are shuffled off with such uncurrent pay.
    But were my worth, as is my conscience, firm,
    You should find better dealing. What's to do?
    Shall we go see the reliques of this town?

ANTONIO

20   Tomorrow, sir; best first go see your lodging.

SEBASTIAN

I am not weary, and 'tis long to night.
I pray you, let us satisfy our eyes
With the memorials and the things of fame
That do renown this city.

ANTONIO

Would you'd pardon me.
I do not without danger walk these streets.
Once in a seafight 'gainst the Count his galleys
I did some service – of such note indeed
That, were I ta'en here, it would scarce be answered.

SEBASTIAN

30   Belike you slew great number of his people?

ANTONIO

Th'offence is not of such a bloody nature,
Albeit the quality of the time and quarrel
Might well have given us bloody argument.
It might have since been answered in repaying
What we took from them, which, for traffic's sake,
Most of our city did. Only myself stood out.
For which, if I be lapsèd in this place,
I shall pay dear.

SEBASTIAN   Do not then walk too open.

ANTONIO

It doth not fit me. Hold, sir, here's my purse.
40   In the south suburbs, at the Elephant,
Is best to lodge. I will bespeak our diet
Whiles you beguile the time, and feed your knowledge
With viewing of the town. There shall you have me.

SEBASTIAN

Why I your purse?

ANTONIO
>   Haply your eye shall light upon some toy
>   You have desire to purchase; and your store,
>   I think, is not for idle markets, sir.

SEBASTIAN
>   I'll be your purse-bearer, and leave you for
>   An hour.

ANTONIO   To th'Elephant.

SEBASTIAN   I do remember.

> *Exeunt separately*

> *Enter Olivia and Maria*   III.4

OLIVIA (*aside*)
>   I have sent after him. He says he'll come:
>   How shall I feast him? What bestow of him?
>   For youth is bought more oft than begged or borrowed.
>   I speak too loud.
>   (*To Maria*) Where's Malvolio? He is sad and civil,
>   And suits well for a servant with my fortunes.
>   Where is Malvolio?

MARIA He's coming, madam, but in very strange manner.
>   He is sure possessed, madam.

OLIVIA Why, what's the matter? Does he rave?   10

MARIA No, madam, he does nothing but smile. Your
>   ladyship were best to have some guard about you, if he
>   come, for sure the man is tainted in's wits.

OLIVIA
>   Go, call him hither.   *Exit Maria*
>   I am as mad as he
>   If sad and merry madness equal be.
>   *Enter Malvolio and Maria*
>   How now, Malvolio?

MALVOLIO Sweet lady! Ho! Ho!

OLIVIA Smil'st thou? I sent for thee upon a sad occasion.

MALVOLIO Sad, lady? I could be sad; this does make
20   some obstruction in the blood, this cross-gartering—but
what of that? If it please the eye of one, it is with me as
the very true sonnet is: 'Please one and please all.'

OLIVIA Why, how dost thou, man? What is the matter
with thee?

MALVOLIO Not black in my mind, though yellow in my
legs. It did come to his hands; and commands shall be
executed. I think we do know the sweet Roman hand.

OLIVIA Wilt thou go to bed, Malvolio?

MALVOLIO To bed! 'Ay, sweetheart, and I'll come to
30   thee!'

OLIVIA God comfort thee! Why dost thou smile so, and
kiss thy hand so oft?

MARIA How do you, Malvolio?

MALVOLIO At your request? Yes; nightingales answer
daws.

MARIA Why appear you with this ridiculous boldness
before my lady?

MALVOLIO 'Be not afraid of greatness.' 'Twas well writ.

OLIVIA What mean'st thou by that, Malvolio?

40   MALVOLIO 'Some are born great —'

OLIVIA Ha?

MALVOLIO 'Some achieve greatness —'

OLIVIA What sayst thou?

MALVOLIO 'And some have greatness thrust upon
them.'

OLIVIA Heaven restore thee!

MALVOLIO 'Remember who commended thy yellow
stockings —'

OLIVIA Thy yellow stockings?

50   MALVOLIO '— and wished to see thee cross-gartered.'

OLIVIA Cross-gartered?

MALVOLIO 'Go to, thou art made if thou desir'st to be
so.'

OLIVIA Am I maid!

MALVOLIO 'If not, let me see thee a servant still.'

OLIVIA Why, this is very midsummer madness.

Enter a Servant

SERVANT Madam, the young gentleman of the Count
Orsino's is returned. I could hardly entreat him back. He
attends your ladyship's pleasure.

OLIVIA I'll come to him.   *Exit Servant*   60
Good Maria, let this fellow be looked to. Where's my
cousin Toby? Let some of my people have a special care
of him. I would not have him miscarry for the half of
my dowry.   *Exeunt Olivia and Maria different ways*

MALVOLIO O ho! Do you come near me now? No worse
man than Sir Toby to look to me! This concurs directly
with the letter. She sends him on purpose, that I may
appear stubborn to him; for she incites me to that in
the letter. 'Cast thy humble slough,' says she. 'Be
opposite with a kinsman, surly with servants, let thy   70
tongue tang with arguments of state, put thyself into the
trick of singularity' – and consequently sets down the
manner how: as, a sad face, a reverend carriage, a slow
tongue, in the habit of some sir of note, and so forth. I
have limed her! But it is Jove's doing, and Jove make me
thankful! And when she went away now – 'let this fellow
be looked to'. Fellow! Not 'Malvolio', nor after my
degree, but 'fellow'! Why, everything adheres together,
that no dram of a scruple, no scruple of a scruple, no
obstacle, no incredulous or unsafe circumstance – what   80
can be said? – nothing that can be, can come between
me and the full prospect of my hopes. Well, Jove, not I,
is the doer of this, and he is to be thanked.

Enter Sir Toby, Fabian, and Maria

SIR TOBY Which way is he, in the name of sanctity? If all
the devils of hell be drawn in little and Legion himself
possessed him, yet I'll speak to him.

FABIAN Here he is, here he is. How is't with you, sir?
How is't with you, man?

MALVOLIO Go off, I discard you. Let me enjoy my private. Go off.

MARIA Lo, how hollow the fiend speaks within him. Did
not I tell you? Sir Toby, my lady prays you to have a
care of him.

MALVOLIO Ah ha! Does she so!

SIR TOBY Go to, go to! Peace, peace, we must deal gently
with him. Let me alone. How do you, Malvolio? How
is't with you? What, man, defy the devil! Consider,
he's an enemy to mankind.

MALVOLIO Do you know what you say?

MARIA La you, an you speak ill of the devil, how he takes
it at heart! Pray God he be not bewitched!

FABIAN Carry his water to the wisewoman.

MARIA Marry, and it shall be done tomorrow morning, if
I live. My lady would not lose him, for more than I'll
say.

MALVOLIO How now, mistress?

MARIA O Lord!

SIR TOBY Prithee, hold thy peace, this is not the way. Do
you not see you move him? Let me alone with him.

FABIAN No way but gentleness, gently, gently. The fiend
is rough, and will not be roughly used.

SIR TOBY Why, how now, my bawcock? How dost thou,
chuck?

MALVOLIO Sir!

SIR TOBY Ay, biddy, come with me. What, man, 'tis not
for gravity to play at cherry-pit with Satan. Hang him,
foul collier!

MARIA Get him to say his prayers, good Sir Toby; get him
to pray.

MALVOLIO My prayers, minx!   120

MARIA No, I warrant you, he will not hear of godliness.

MALVOLIO Go, hang yourselves all. You are idle, shallow
things; I am not of your element. You shall know more
hereafter.   *Exit Malvolio*

SIR TOBY Is't possible?

FABIAN If this were played upon a stage now, I could
condemn it as an improbable fiction.

SIR TOBY His very genius hath taken the infection of the
device, man.

MARIA Nay, pursue him now, lest the device take air, and   130
taint.

FABIAN Why, we shall make him mad indeed.

MARIA The house will be the quieter.

SIR TOBY Come, we'll have him in a dark room and
bound. My niece is already in the belief that he's mad.
We may carry it thus for our pleasure and his penance
till our very pastime, tired out of breath, prompt us to
have mercy on him; at which time, we will bring the
device to the bar, and crown thee for a finder of madmen. But see, but see!   140

    Enter Sir Andrew

FABIAN More matter for a May morning!

SIR ANDREW Here's the challenge, read it. I warrant
there's vinegar and pepper in't.

FABIAN Is't so saucy?

SIR ANDREW Ay, is't, I warrant him. Do but read.

SIR TOBY Give me.

    He reads
    Youth, whatsoever thou art, thou art but a scurvy fellow.

FABIAN Good and valiant.

SIR TOBY (*reads*) *Wonder not, nor admire not in thy mind,*

150 *why I do call thee so, for I will show thee no reason for't.*

FABIAN A good note, that keeps you from the blow of the law.

SIR TOBY (*reads*) *Thou com'st to the Lady Olivia, and in my sight she uses thee kindly. But thou liest in thy throat; that is not the matter I challenge thee for.*

FABIAN Very brief, and to exceeding good sense — (*aside*) less!

SIR TOBY (*reads*) *I will waylay thee going home; where, if it be thy chance to kill me —*

160 FABIAN Good!

SIR TOBY (*reads*) *thou kill'st me like a rogue and a villain.*

FABIAN Still you keep o' the windy side of the law; good.

SIR TOBY (*reads*) *Fare thee well, and God have mercy upon one of our souls. He may have mercy upon mine, but my hope is better — and so, look to thyself. Thy friend as thou usest him, and thy sworn enemy, Andrew Aguecheek.* If this letter move him not, his legs cannot. I'll give 't him.

170 MARIA You may have very fit occasion for't. He is now in some commerce with my lady, and will by and by depart.

SIR TOBY Go, Sir Andrew. Scout me for him at the corner of the orchard like a bum-baily. So soon as ever thou seest him, draw, and as thou drawest, swear horrible; for it comes to pass oft that a terrible oath, with a swaggering accent sharply twanged off, gives manhood more approbation than ever proof itself would have earned him. Away!

180 SIR ANDREW Nay, let me alone for swearing.   *Exit*

SIR TOBY Now will not I deliver his letter. For the behaviour of the young gentleman gives him out to be of good capacity and breeding; his employment between

his lord and my niece confirms no less. Therefore this
letter, being so excellently ignorant, will breed no terror
in the youth; he will find it comes from a clodpole. But,
sir, I will deliver his challenge by word of mouth; set
upon Aguecheek a notable report of valour, and drive
the gentleman — as I know his youth will aptly receive it
— into a most hideous opinion of his rage, skill, fury, and
impetuosity. This will so fright them both, that they   190
will kill one another by the look, like cockatrices.
        Enter Olivia and Viola
FABIAN Here he comes with your niece. Give them way
    till he take leave, and presently after him.
SIR TOBY I will meditate the while upon some horrid
    message for a challenge.
                                          Exit Maria
        Sir Toby and Fabian stand aside
OLIVIA
    I have said too much unto a heart of stone,
    And laid mine honour too unchary on't.
    There's something in me that reproves my fault.
    But such a headstrong, potent fault it is,   200
    That it but mocks reproof.
VIOLA
    With the same 'haviour that your passion bears
    Goes on my master's griefs.
OLIVIA
    Here, wear this jewel for me, 'tis my picture.
    Refuse it not, it hath no tongue to vex you.
    And, I beseech you, come again tomorrow.
    What shall you ask of me that I'll deny,
    That honour saved may upon asking give?
VIOLA
    Nothing but this: your true love for my master.

OLIVIA

210   How with mine honour may I give him that
       Which I have given to you?

VIOLA   I will acquit you.

OLIVIA

       Well, come again tomorrow. Fare thee well.
       A fiend like thee might bear my soul to hell.   *Exit*
          Sir Toby and Fabian come forward

SIR TOBY Gentleman, God save thee!

VIOLA And you, sir.

SIR TOBY That defence thou hast, betake thee to't. Of
       what nature the wrongs are thou hast done him, I know
       not; but thy intercepter, full of despite, bloody as the
       hunter, attends thee at the orchard end. Dismount thy
220   tuck; be yare in thy preparation; for thy assailant is
       quick, skilful, and deadly.

VIOLA You mistake, sir. I am sure no man hath any
       quarrel to me. My remembrance is very free and clear
       from any image of offence done to any man.

SIR TOBY You'll find it otherwise, I assure you. There-
       fore, if you hold your life at any price, betake you to
       your guard; for your opposite hath in him what youth,
       strength, skill, and wrath can furnish man withal.

VIOLA I pray you, sir, what is he?

230   SIR TOBY He is knight dubbed with unhatched rapier and
       on carpet consideration – but he is a devil in private
       brawl. Souls and bodies hath he divorced three; and his
       incensement at this moment is so implacable, that satis-
       faction can be none, but by pangs of death, and se-
       pulchre. Hob, nob! is his word: give't or take't.

VIOLA I will return again into the house and desire some
       conduct of the lady. I am no fighter. I have heard of
       some kind of men that put quarrels purposely on others
       to taste their valour. Belike this is a man of that quirk.

SIR TOBY Sir, no. His indignation derives itself out of a   240
very computent injury. Therefore, get you on and give
him his desire. Back you shall not to the house, unless
you undertake that with me, which with as much safety
you might answer him. Therefore on, or strip your
sword stark naked; for meddle you must, that's certain,
or forswear to wear iron about you.

VIOLA This is as uncivil as strange. I beseech you, do me
this courteous office, as to know of the knight what my
offence to him is. It is something of my negligence,
nothing of my purpose.   250

SIR TOBY I will do so. Signor Fabian, stay you by this
gentleman till my return.   *Exit*

VIOLA Pray you, sir, do you know of this matter?

FABIAN I know the knight is incensed against you, even
to a mortal arbitrement, but nothing of the circumstance
more.

VIOLA I beseech you, what manner of man is he?

FABIAN Nothing of that wonderful promise, to read him
by his form, as you are like to find him in the proof
of his valour. He is indeed, sir, the most skilful, bloody,   260
and fatal opposite that you could possibly have found in
any part of Illyria. Will you walk towards him? I will
make your peace with him, if I can.

VIOLA I shall be much bound to you for't. I am one that
had rather go with Sir Priest than Sir Knight; I care not
who knows so much of my mettle.

Enter Sir Toby and Sir Andrew

SIR TOBY Why, man, he's a very devil. I have not seen
such a firago. I had a pass with him, rapier, scabbard
and all; and he gives me the stuck-in with such a mortal
motion that it is inevitable; and on the answer, he pays   270
you as surely as your feet hits the ground they step on.
They say he has been fencer to the Sophy.

SIR ANDREW Pox on't! I'll not meddle with him.

SIR TOBY Ay, but he will not now be pacified. Fabian can scarce hold him yonder.

SIR ANDREW Plague on't! An I thought he had been valiant, and so cunning in fence, I'd have seen him damned ere I'd have challenged him. Let him let the matter slip, and I'll give him my horse, grey Capilet.

280 SIR TOBY I'll make the motion. Stand here, make a good show on't. This shall end without the perdition of souls. (*Aside, as he crosses to Fabian*) Marry, I'll ride your horse as well as I ride you! (*To Fabian*) I have his horse to take up the quarrel. I have persuaded him the youth's a devil.

FABIAN He is as horribly conceited of him, and pants and looks pale as if a bear were at his heels.

SIR TOBY (*to Viola*) There's no remedy, sir, he will fight with you for's oath's sake. Marry, he hath better be-
290 thought him of his quarrel, and he finds that now scarce to be worth talking of. Therefore, draw for the sup-portance of his vow. He protests he will not hurt you.

VIOLA (*aside*) Pray God defend me! A little thing would make me tell them how much I lack of a man.

FABIAN Give ground if you see him furious.

SIR TOBY (*crossing to Sir Andrew*) Come, Sir Andrew, there's no remedy. The gentleman will, for his honour's sake, have one bout with you, he cannot by the *duello* avoid it. But he has promised me, as he is a gentleman
300 and a soldier, he will not hurt you. Come on, to't!

SIR ANDREW Pray God he keep his oath!

He draws
Enter Antonio

VIOLA I do assure you, 'tis against my will.
She draws

ANTONIO
> Put up your sword. If this young gentleman
> Have done offence, I take the fault on me.
> If you offend him, I for him defy you.

SIR TOBY You, sir? Why, what are you?

ANTONIO
> One, sir, that for his love dares yet do more
> Than you have heard him brag to you he will.

SIR TOBY Nay, if you be an undertaker, I am for you.
> *Enter Officers*

FABIAN O good Sir Toby, hold! Here come the Officers.   310

SIR TOBY (*to Antonio*) I'll be with you anon.

VIOLA (*to Sir Andrew*) Pray sir, put your sword up, if
you please.

SIR ANDREW Marry, will I, sir. And for that I promised
you, I'll be as good as my word. He will bear you easily,
and reins well.

FIRST OFFICER This is the man; do thy office.

SECOND OFFICER
> Antonio, I arrest thee at the suit
> Of Count Orsino.

ANTONIO   You do mistake me, sir.

FIRST OFFICER
> No, sir, no jot. I know your favour well,   320
> Though now you have no sea-cap on your head.
> Take him away; he knows I know him well.

ANTONIO
> I must obey. (*To Viola*) This comes with seeking you.
> But there's no remedy, I shall answer it.
> What will you do, now my necessity
> Makes me to ask you for my purse? It grieves me
> Much more for what I cannot do for you
> Than what befalls myself. You stand amazed;
> But be of comfort.

SECOND OFFICER   Come, sir, away!

330   ANTONIO I must entreat of you some of that money.

VIOLA
        What money, sir?
        For the fair kindness you have showed me here,
        And part being prompted by your present trouble,
        Out of my lean and low ability,
        I'll lend you something. My having is not much.
        I'll make division of my present with you.
        Hold: there's half my coffer.

ANTONIO
        Will you deny me now?
        Is't possible that my deserts to you
340   Can lack persuasion? Do not tempt my misery,
        Lest that it make me so unsound a man
        As to upbraid you with those kindnesses
        That I have done for you.

VIOLA   I know of none.
        Nor know I you by voice or any feature.
        I hate ingratitude more in a man
        Than lying, vainness, babbling drunkenness,
        Or any taint of vice whose strong corruption
        Inhabits our frail blood —

ANTONIO   O heavens themselves!

SECOND OFFICER
        Come, sir, I pray you go.

ANTONIO
350   Let me speak a little. This youth that you see here
        I snatched one half out of the jaws of death;
        Relieved him with such sanctity of love;
        And to his image, which methought did promise
        Most venerable worth, did I devotion.

FIRST OFFICER
        What's that to us? The time goes by. Away!

ANTONIO

   But O, how vild an idol proves this god!
   Thou hast, Sebastian, done good feature shame.
   In nature, there's no blemish but the mind;
   None can be called deformed, but the unkind.
   Virtue is beauty; but the beauteous evil   360
   Are empty trunks o'er-flourished by the devil.

FIRST OFFICER

   The man grows mad; away with him. Come, come, sir.

ANTONIO

   Lead me on.   *Exeunt Antonio and Officers*

VIOLA (*aside*)

   Methinks his words do from such passion fly
   That he believes himself; so do not I?
   Prove true, imagination, O, prove true –
   That I, dear brother, be now ta'en for you!

SIR TOBY Come hither, knight; come hither, Fabian.
   We'll whisper o'er a couplet or two of most sage saws.

VIOLA

   He named Sebastian. I my brother know   370
   Yet living in my glass. Even such and so
   In favour was my brother; and he went
   Still in this fashion, colour, ornament,
   For him I imitate. O, if it prove,
   Tempests are kind, and salt waves fresh in love! *Exit*

SIR TOBY A very dishonest, paltry boy, and more a
   coward than a hare. His dishonesty appears in leaving
   his friend here in necessity and denying him; and for his
   cowardship, ask Fabian.

FABIAN A coward, a most devout coward, religious in it!   380

SIR ANDREW 'Slid! I'll after him again and beat him.

SIR TOBY Do, cuff him soundly, but never draw thy
   sword.

SIR ANDREW An I do not –   *Exit*

FABIAN Come, let's see the event.

SIR TOBY I dare lay any money, 'twill be nothing yet.

Exeunt

*

IV.1   *Enter Sebastian and Feste*

FESTE Will you make me believe that I am not sent for
you?

SEBASTIAN Go to, go to, thou art a foolish fellow. Let me
be clear of thee.

FESTE Well held out, i'faith. No: I do not know you; nor
I am not sent to you by my lady, to bid you come speak
with her; nor your name is not Master Cesario; nor this
is not my nose, neither. Nothing that is so, is so.

SEBASTIAN I prithee, vent thy folly somewhere else; thou
10   knowest not me.

FESTE Vent my folly! He has heard that word of some
great man, and now applies it to a fool. Vent my folly!
I am afraid this great lubber the world will prove a
cockney. I prithee now, ungird thy strangeness, and
tell me what I shall vent to my lady? Shall I vent to her
that thou art coming?

SEBASTIAN I prithee, foolish Greek, depart from me.
There's money for thee; if you tarry longer, I shall give
worse payment.

20   FESTE By my troth, thou hast an open hand! These wise
men that give fools money get themselves a good report
– after fourteen years' purchase.

Enter Sir Andrew, Sir Toby, and Fabian

SIR ANDREW Now, sir, have I met you again? There's
for you!

He strikes Sebastian

SEBASTIAN Why, there's for thee! And there!
> *He beats Sir Andrew with the handle of his dagger*
And there! Are all the people mad?

SIR TOBY Hold, sir, or I'll throw your dagger o'er the house.

FESTE This will I tell my lady straight. I would not be in some of your coats, for twopence.   *Exit* 30

SIR TOBY Come on, sir, hold!
> *He grips Sebastian*

SIR ANDREW Nay, let him alone. I'll go another way to work with him. I'll have an action of battery against him, if there be any law in Illyria — though I struck him first, yet it's no matter for that.

SEBASTIAN Let go thy hand!

SIR TOBY Come, sir, I will not let you go. Come, my young soldier, put up your iron; you are well fleshed. Come on!

SEBASTIAN
I will be free from thee!
> *He breaks free and draws his sword*
                              What wouldst thou now? 40
If thou darest tempt me further, draw thy sword.

SIR TOBY What, what! Nay, then, I must have an ounce or two of this malapert blood from you.
> *He draws*
> *Enter Olivia*

OLIVIA
Hold, Toby! On thy life, I charge thee hold!

SIR TOBY Madam!

OLIVIA
Will it be ever thus? Ungracious wretch,
Fit for the mountains and the barbarous caves
Where manners ne'er were preached, out of my sight!
Be not offended, dear Cesario.

50   Rudesby, be gone!
                    Exeunt Sir Toby, Sir Andrew, and Fabian
                              I prithee, gentle friend,
         Let thy fair wisdom, not thy passion, sway
         In this uncivil and unjust extent
         Against thy peace. Go with me to my house,
         And hear thou there how many fruitless pranks
         This ruffian hath botched up, that thou thereby
         Mayst smile at this. Thou shalt not choose but go;
         Do not deny. Beshrew his soul for me!
         He started one poor heart of mine, in thee.
    SEBASTIAN (*aside*)
         What relish is in this? How runs the stream?
60   Or I am mad, or else this is a dream.
         Let fancy still my sense in Lethe steep;
         If it be thus to dream, still let me sleep!
    OLIVIA
         Nay, come, I prithee. Would thou'dst be ruled by me!
    SEBASTIAN
         Madam, I will.
    OLIVIA   O, say so, and so be!   *Exeunt*

IV.2   *Enter Maria and Feste*
    MARIA Nay, I prithee, put on this gown and this beard;
         make him believe thou art Sir Topas the curate. Do it
         quickly. I'll call Sir Toby the whilst.   *Exit*
    FESTE Well, I'll put it on and I will dissemble myself in't,
         and I would I were the first that ever dissembled in such
         a gown. I am not tall enough to become the function
         well, nor lean enough to be thought a good student. But
         to be said an honest man and a good housekeeper goes as
         fairly as to say a careful man and a great scholar. The
10   competitors enter.

Enter Sir Toby and Maria

SIR TOBY Jove bless thee, Master Parson!

FESTE *Bonos dies*, Sir Toby; for as the old hermit of
Prague that never saw pen and ink very wittily said to
a niece of King Gorboduc: that that is, is. So I, being
Master Parson, am Master Parson; for what is 'that' but
'that'? And 'is' but 'is'?

SIR TOBY To him, Sir Topas.

FESTE What ho, I say! Peace in this prison!

SIR TOBY The knave counterfeits well; a good knave.

MALVOLIO (*within*) Who calls there?   20

FESTE Sir Topas the curate, who comes to visit Malvolio
the lunatic.

MALVOLIO Sir Topas, Sir Topas, good Sir Topas, go to
my lady —

FESTE Out, hyperbolical fiend, how vexest thou this man!
Talkest thou nothing but of ladies?

SIR TOBY Well said, Master Parson.

MALVOLIO Sir Topas, never was man thus wronged.
Good Sir Topas, do not think I am mad. They have laid
me here in hideous darkness —   30

FESTE Fie, thou dishonest Satan! I call thee by the most
modest terms, for I am one of those gentle ones that will
use the devil himself with courtesy. Sayst thou that
house is dark?

MALVOLIO As hell, Sir Topas.

FESTE Why, it hath bay windows transparent as barricadoes, and the clerestories toward the south–north
are as lustrous as ebony. And yet complainest thou of
obstruction!

MALVOLIO I am not mad, Sir Topas. I say to you, this   40
house is dark.

FESTE Madman, thou errest. I say there is no darkness but
ignorance, in which thou art more puzzled than the
Egyptians in their fog.

MALVOLIO I say this house is as dark as ignorance, though ignorance were as dark as hell. And I say there was never man thus abused. I am no more mad than you are – make the trial of it in any constant question.

FESTE What is the opinion of Pythagoras concerning
50   wildfowl?

MALVOLIO That the soul of our grandam might haply inhabit a bird.

FESTE What thinkest thou of his opinion?

MALVOLIO I think nobly of the soul, and no way approve his opinion.

FESTE Fare thee well; remain thou still in darkness. Thou shalt hold the opinion of Pythagoras ere I will allow of thy wits, and fear to kill a woodcock lest thou dispossess the soul of thy grandam. Fare thee well.

60 MALVOLIO Sir Topas, Sir Topas!

SIR TOBY My most exquisite Sir Topas!

FESTE Nay, I am for all waters.

MARIA Thou mightst have done this without thy beard and gown; he sees thee not.

SIR TOBY To him in thine own voice, and bring me word how thou findest him. I would we were well rid of this knavery. If he may be conveniently delivered, I would he were, for I am now so far in offence with my niece that I cannot pursue with any safety this sport the up-
70   shot. Come by and by to my chamber.

Exeunt Sir Toby and Maria

FESTE (*sings*)
　　　　　Hey Robin, jolly Robin!
　　　　　Tell me how thy lady does –

MALVOLIO Fool!

FESTE (*sings*)
　　　　　My lady is unkind, perdy.

MALVOLIO Fool!

FESTE (*sings*)
>   Alas, why is she so?

MALVOLIO Fool, I say!

FESTE (*sings*)
>   She loves another —

Who calls, ha?

MALVOLIO Good fool, as ever thou wilt deserve well at   80
my hand, help me to a candle, and pen, ink, and paper.
As I am a gentleman, I will live to be thankful to thee
for't.

FESTE Master Malvolio?

MALVOLIO Ay, good fool.

FESTE Alas, sir, how fell you besides your five wits?

MALVOLIO Fool, there was never man so notoriously
abused. I am as well in my wits, fool, as thou art.

FESTE But as well? Then you are mad indeed, if you be
no better in your wits than a fool.   90

MALVOLIO They have here propertied me; keep me in
darkness, send ministers to me — asses! — and do all they
can to face me out of my wits.

FESTE Advise you what you say. The minister is here.
(*In priest's voice*) Malvolio, Malvolio, thy wits the
heavens restore! Endeavour thyself to sleep and leave
thy vain bibble-babble.

MALVOLIO Sir Topas!

FESTE Maintain no words with him, good fellow. (*In own
voice*) Who, I, sir? Not I, sir! God buy you, good Sir   100
Topas! (*In priest's voice*) Marry, amen! (*In own voice*)
I will, sir, I will.

MALVOLIO Fool! Fool! Fool, I say!

FESTE Alas, sir, be patient. What say you sir? I am shent
for speaking to you.

MALVOLIO Good fool, help me to some light and some
paper. I tell thee, I am as well in my wits as any man in
Illyria.

FESTE Well-a-day, that you were, sir!

110 MALVOLIO By this hand, I am! Good fool, some ink, paper, and light; and convey what I will set down to my lady. It shall advantage thee more than ever the bearing of letter did.

FESTE I will help you to't. But tell me true, are you not mad indeed, or do you but counterfeit?

MALVOLIO Believe me, I am not. I tell thee true.

FESTE Nay, I'll ne'er believe a madman till I see his brains. I will fetch you light, and paper, and ink.

MALVOLIO Fool, I'll requite it in the highest degree. I
120 prithee, be gone.

FESTE (*sings*)

    I am gone, sir, and anon, sir,
        I'll be with you again.
    In a trice, like to the old Vice,
        Your need to sustain.
    Who with dagger of lath, in his rage and his
        wrath,
        Cries 'Ah ha!' to the devil;
    Like a mad lad – 'Pare thy nails, dad?
        Adieu, goodman devil!'   *Exit*

IV.3   *Enter Sebastian*

SEBASTIAN

    This is the air; that is the glorious sun;
    This pearl she gave me, I do feel't and see't;
    And though 'tis wonder that enwraps me thus,
    Yet 'tis not madness. Where's Antonio, then?
    I could not find him at the Elephant.
    Yet there he was; and there I found this credit
    That he did range the town to seek me out.
    His counsel now might do me golden service.

For though my soul disputes well with my sense
That this may be some error, but no madness,   10
Yet doth this accident and flood of fortune
So far exceed all instance, all discourse,
That I am ready to distrust mine eyes,
And wrangle with my reason that persuades me
To any other trust but that I am mad –
Or else the lady's mad; yet if 'twere so,
She could not sway her house, command her followers,
Take and give back affairs and their dispatch,
With such a smooth, discreet, and stable bearing
As I perceive she does. There's something in't   20
That is deceivable. But here the lady comes.

    Enter Olivia and a Priest

OLIVIA
Blame not this haste of mine. If you mean well,
Now go with me and with this holy man
Into the chantry by; there before him
And underneath that consecrated roof
Plight me the full assurance of your faith,
That my most jealous and too doubtful soul
May live at peace. He shall conceal it
Whiles you are willing it shall come to note;
What time we will our celebration keep   30
According to my birth. What do you say?

SEBASTIAN
I'll follow this good man, and go with you;
And having sworn truth, ever will be true.

OLIVIA
Then lead the way, good father, and heavens so shine
That they may fairly note this act of mine!   *Exeunt*

*

V. I   *Enter Feste and Fabian*

FABIAN Now, as thou lov'st me, let me see his letter.

FESTE Good Master Fabian, grant me another request.

FABIAN Anything!

FESTE Do not desire to see this letter.

FABIAN This is to give a dog, and in recompense desire
my dog again.

Enter Orsino, Viola, Curio, and lords

ORSINO Belong you to the Lady Olivia, friends?

FESTE Ay, sir, we are some of her trappings.

ORSINO I know thee well. How dost thou, my good
10   fellow?

FESTE Truly, sir, the better for my foes, and the worse for
my friends.

ORSINO Just the contrary: the better for thy friends.

FESTE No, sir: the worse.

ORSINO How can that be?

FESTE Marry, sir, they praise me – and make an ass of me.
Now my foes tell me plainly, I am an ass; so that by my
foes, sir, I profit in the knowledge of myself, and by my
friends I am abused. So that, conclusions to be as
20   kisses, if your four negatives make your two affirma-
tives, why then, the worse for my friends and the better
for my foes.

ORSINO Why, this is excellent.

FESTE By my troth, sir, no – though it please you to be
one of my friends.

ORSINO Thou shalt not be the worse for me: there's gold.

FESTE But that it would be double-dealing, sir, I would
you could make it another.

ORSINO O, you give me ill counsel!

30   FESTE Put your grace in your pocket, sir, for this once,
and let your flesh and blood obey it.

ORSINO Well, I will be so much a sinner to be a double-dealer; there's another.

FESTE *Primo, secundo, tertio,* is a good play; and the old
saying is, the third pays for all; the triplex, sir, is a good
tripping measure; or the bells of Saint Bennet, sir, may
put you in mind — one, two, three!

ORSINO You can fool no more money out of me at this
throw. If you will let your lady know I am here to speak
with her, and bring her along with you, it may awake my   40
bounty further.

FESTE Marry, sir, lullaby to your bounty till I come
again. I go, sir, but I would not have you to think that
my desire of having is the sin of covetousness. But as
you say, sir, let your bounty take a nap — I will awake it
anon.   *Exit*

    Enter Antonio and Officers

VIOLA
Here comes the man, sir, that did rescue me.

ORSINO
That face of his I do remember well.
Yet when I saw it last, it was besmeared
As black as Vulcan in the smoke of war.   50
A baubling vessel was he captain of,
For shallow draught and bulk, unprizable;
With which, such scatheful grapple did he make
With the most noble bottom of our fleet,
That very envy and the tongue of loss
Cried fame and honour on him. What's the matter?

FIRST OFFICER
Orsino, this is that Antonio
That took the *Phoenix*, and her fraught from Candy;
And this is he that did the *Tiger* board
When your young nephew Titus lost his leg.   60
Here in the streets, desperate of shame and state,
In private brabble did we apprehend him.

VIOLA

> He did me kindness, sir, drew on my side,
> But in conclusion put strange speech upon me.
> I know not what 'twas, but distraction.

ORSINO

> Notable pirate, thou salt-water thief,
> What foolish boldness brought thee to their mercies
> Whom thou, in terms so bloody and so dear,
> Hast made thine enemies?

ANTONIO

70 > Orsino, noble sir,
> Be pleased that I shake off these names you give me.
> Antonio never yet was thief or pirate;
> Though, I confess, on base and ground enough,
> Orsino's enemy. A witchcraft drew me hither.
> That most ingrateful boy there by your side
> From the rude sea's enraged and foamy mouth
> Did I redeem; a wrack past hope he was.
> His life I gave him, and did thereto add
> My love without retention or restraint,
80 > All his in dedication. For his sake
> Did I expose myself – pure for his love –
> Into the danger of this adverse town;
> Drew to defend him when he was beset;
> Where, being apprehended, his false cunning –
> Not meaning to partake with me in danger –
> Taught him to face me out of his acquaintance,
> And grew a twenty years' removèd thing
> While one would wink; denied me mine own purse
> Which I had recommended to his use
90 > Not half an hour before.

VIOLA   How can this be?

ORSINO

> When came he to this town?

ANTONIO

Today, my lord; and for three months before
No interim, not a minute's vacancy,
Both day and night, did we keep company.

Enter Olivia and attendants

ORSINO

Here comes the Countess; now heaven walks on earth!
But for thee, fellow — fellow, thy words are madness.
Three months this youth hath tended upon me.
But more of that anon. Take him aside.

OLIVIA

What would my lord — but that he may not have —
Wherein Olivia may seem serviceable?   100
Cesario, you do not keep promise with me.

VIOLA

Madam?

ORSINO

Gracious Olivia —

OLIVIA

What do you say, Cesario? (*To Orsino*) Good, my lord.

VIOLA

My lord would speak; my duty hushes me.

OLIVIA

If it be aught to the old tune, my lord,
It is as fat and fulsome to mine ear
As howling after music.

ORSINO

Still so cruel?

OLIVIA   Still so constant, lord.

ORSINO

What, to perverseness? You uncivil lady,   110
To whose ingrate and unauspicious altars
My soul the faithfull'st offerings have breathed out
That e'er devotion tendered! What shall I do?

OLIVIA

Even what it please my lord, that shall become him.

ORSINO

Why should I not — had I the heart to do it —
Like to th'Egyptian thief at point of death
Kill what I love — a savage jealousy
That sometime savours nobly? But hear me this:
Since you to non-regardance cast my faith,
120   And that I partly know the instrument
That screws me from my true place in your favour,
Live you the marble-breasted tyrant still.
But this your minion, whom I know you love,
And whom, by heaven, I swear, I tender dearly,
Him will I tear out of that cruel eye
Where he sits crownèd in his master's spite.
Come, boy, with me, my thoughts are ripe in mischief.
I'll sacrifice the lamb that I do love
To spite a raven's heart within a dove.

VIOLA

130   And I, most jocund, apt, and willingly
To do you rest, a thousand deaths would die.

OLIVIA

Where goes Cesario?

VIOLA   After him I love
More than I love these eyes, more than my life,
More by all mores than e'er I shall love wife.
If I do feign, you witnesses above,
Punish my life, for tainting of my love!

OLIVIA

Ay me, detested! How am I beguiled!

VIOLA

Who does beguile you? Who does do you wrong?

OLIVIA

Hast thou forgot thyself? Is it so long?

Call forth the holy father!   *Exit an attendant*

ORSINO   Come, away!   140

OLIVIA

Whither, my lord? Cesario, husband, stay!

ORSINO

Husband?

OLIVIA   Ay, husband. Can he that deny?

ORSINO

Her husband, sirrah?

VIOLA   No, my lord, not I.

OLIVIA

Alas, it is the baseness of thy fear
That makes thee strangle thy propriety.
Fear not, Cesario, take thy fortunes up.
Be that thou know'st thou art, and then thou art
As great as that thou fear'st.

     Enter Priest

                              O, welcome, Father.
Father, I charge thee, by thy reverence,
Here to unfold – though lately we intended   150
To keep in darkness what occasion now
Reveals before 'tis ripe – what thou dost know
Hath newly passed between this youth and me.

PRIEST

A contract of eternal bond of love,
Confirmed by mutual joinder of your hands,
Attested by the holy close of lips,
Strengthened by interchangement of your rings,
And all the ceremony of this compact
Sealed in my function, by my testimony;
Since when, my watch hath told me, toward my grave   160
I have travelled but two hours.

ORSINO

O thou dissembling cub! What wilt thou be

When time hath sowed a grizzle on thy case?
Or will not else thy craft so quickly grow
That thine own trip shall be thine overthrow?
Farewell, and take her; but direct thy feet
Where thou and I henceforth may never meet.

VIOLA
My lord, I do protest —

OLIVIA   O, do not swear!
Hold little faith, though thou hast too much fear.
Enter Sir Andrew

170 SIR ANDREW For the love of God, a surgeon! Send one
presently to Sir Toby.

OLIVIA What's the matter?

SIR ANDREW He's broke my head across, and he's given
Sir Toby a bloody coxcomb too. For the love of God,
your help! I had rather than forty pound I were at home.

OLIVIA Who has done this, Sir Andrew?

SIR ANDREW The Count's gentleman, one Cesario. We
took him for a coward, but he's the very devil incardinate.

180 ORSINO My gentleman, Cesario?

SIR ANDREW 'Od's lifelings, here he is! You broke my
head for nothing; and that that I did, I was set on to do't
by Sir Toby.

VIOLA
Why do you speak to me? I never hurt you.
You drew your sword upon me without cause,
But I bespake you fair, and hurt you not.
Enter Sir Toby and Feste

SIR ANDREW If a bloody coxcomb be a hurt, you have
hurt me. I think you set nothing by a bloody coxcomb.
Here comes Sir Toby halting, you shall hear more; but
190 if he had not been in drink, he would have tickled you
othergates than he did.

ORSINO How now, gentleman? How is't with you?

SIR TOBY That's all one; he's hurt me, and there's the end
on't. (*To Feste*) Sot, didst see Dick Surgeon, sot?

FESTE O, he's drunk, Sir Toby, an hour agone. His eyes
were set at eight i'the morning.

SIR TOBY Then he's a rogue and a passy-measures pavin.
I hate a drunken rogue.

OLIVIA Away with him! Who hath made this havoc with
them?   200

SIR ANDREW I'll help you, Sir Toby, because we'll be
dressed together.

SIR TOBY Will you help? An asshead, and a coxcomb,
and a knave – a thin-faced knave, a gull!

OLIVIA Get him to bed, and let his hurt be looked to.

Exeunt Sir Toby and Sir Andrew,
helped by Feste and Fabian

Enter Sebastian

SEBASTIAN

I am sorry, madam, I have hurt your kinsman.
But had it been the brother of my blood
I must have done no less, with wit and safety.
You throw a strange regard upon me; and by that
I do perceive it hath offended you.   210
Pardon me, sweet one, even for the vows
We made each other but so late ago.

ORSINO

One face, one voice, one habit, and two persons!
A natural perspective, that is and is not.

SEBASTIAN

Antonio! O, my dear Antonio!
How have the hours racked and tortured me
Since I have lost thee!

ANTONIO

Sebastian, are you?

SEBASTIAN   Fear'st thou that, Antonio?
ANTONIO
How have you made division of yourself?
220   An apple cleft in two is not more twin
Than these two creatures. Which is Sebastian?
OLIVIA
Most wonderful!
SEBASTIAN
Do I stand there? I never had a brother;
Nor can there be that deity in my nature
Of here and everywhere. I had a sister
Whom the blind waves and surges have devoured.
Of charity, what kin are you to me?
What countryman? What name? What parentage?
VIOLA
Of Messaline. Sebastian was my father.
230   Such a Sebastian was my brother too.
So went he suited to his watery tomb.
If spirits can assume both form and suit
You come to fright us.
SEBASTIAN   A spirit I am indeed,
But am in that dimension grossly clad
Which from the womb I did participate.
Were you a woman, as the rest goes even,
I should my tears let fall upon your cheek,
And say, 'Thrice welcome, drownèd Viola.'
VIOLA
My father had a mole upon his brow.
SEBASTIAN
240   And so had mine.
VIOLA
And died that day when Viola from her birth
Had numbered thirteen years.

SEBASTIAN
    O, that record is lively in my soul.
    He finishèd indeed his mortal act
    That day that made my sister thirteen years.

VIOLA
    If nothing lets to make us happy both
    But this my masculine usurped attire,
    Do not embrace me, till each circumstance
    Of place, time, fortune, do cohere and jump
    That I am Viola; which to confirm,   250
    I'll bring you to a captain in this town
    Where lie my maiden weeds; by whose gentle help
    I was preserved to serve this noble Count.
    All the occurrence of my fortune since
    Hath been between this lady and this lord.

SEBASTIAN (*to Olivia*)
    So comes it, lady, you have been mistook.
    But nature to her bias drew in that.
    You would have been contracted to a maid.
    Nor are you therein, by my life, deceived:
    You are betrothed both to a maid and man.   260

ORSINO
    Be not amazed; right noble is his blood.
    If this be so, as yet the glass seems true,
    I shall have share in this most happy wrack.
    (*To Viola*) Boy, thou hast said to me a thousand times
    Thou never shouldst love woman like to me.

VIOLA
    And all those sayings will I overswear
    And all those swearings keep as true in soul
    As doth that orbèd continent the fire
    That severs day from night.

ORSINO   Give me thy hand,
    And let me see thee in thy woman's weeds.   270

VIOLA

The Captain that did bring me first on shore
Hath my maid's garments. He, upon some action,
Is now in durance at Malvolio's suit,
A gentleman and follower of my lady's.

OLIVIA

He shall enlarge him; fetch Malvolio hither.
And yet, alas, now I remember me,
They say, poor gentleman, he's much distract.
            Enter Feste with a letter, and Fabian
A most extracting frenzy of mine own
From my remembrance clearly banished his.

280   (*To Feste*) How does he, sirrah?

FESTE Truly, madam, he holds Beelzebub at the stave's
end as well as a man in his case may do. He's here writ a
letter to you. I should have given it you today morning.
But as a madman's epistles are no gospels, so it skills not
much when they are delivered.

OLIVIA Open it, and read it.

FESTE Look, then, to be well edified when the fool delivers the madman.
            He reads frantically

            By the Lord, madam —

290 OLIVIA How now, art thou mad?

FESTE No, madam; I do but read madness. An your
ladyship will have it as it ought to be, you must allow
vox.

OLIVIA Prithee, read i'thy right wits.

FESTE So I do, madonna; but to read his right wits, is to
read thus. Therefore, perpend, my princess, and give
ear.

OLIVIA (*snatching the letter and giving it to Fabian*) Read
it you, sirrah.

FABIAN (*reads*)

By the Lord, madam, you wrong me, and the world shall 300
know it. Though you have put me into darkness and given
your drunken cousin rule over me, yet have I the benefit of
my senses as well as your ladyship. I have your own letter
that induced me to the semblance I put on; with the which
I doubt not but to do myself much right, or you much
shame. Think of me as you please, I leave my duty a little
unthought-of, and speak out of my injury. The madly-used
Malvolio.

OLIVIA Did he write this?
FESTE Ay, madam.   310
ORSINO This savours not much of distraction.
OLIVIA
See him delivered, Fabian, bring him hither.
                                        Exit Fabian
My lord, so please you, these things further thought on,
To think me as well a sister as a wife,
One day shall crown th'alliance on't, so please you,
Here at my house, and at my proper cost.
ORSINO
Madam, I am most apt t'embrace your offer.
(*To Viola*) Your master quits you; and for your service
      done him
So much against the mettle of your sex,
So far beneath your soft and tender breeding,   320
And since you called me master for so long,
Here is my hand; you shall from this time be
Your master's mistress.
OLIVIA   A sister, you are she.
      Enter Malvolio and Fabian

ORSINO
  Is this the madman?
OLIVIA   Ay, my lord, this same.
  How now, Malvolio?
MALVOLIO
  Madam, you have done me wrong;
  Notorious wrong.
OLIVIA   Have I, Malvolio? No!
MALVOLIO
  Lady, you have; pray you, peruse that letter.
  You must not now deny it is your hand.
330 Write from it if you can, in hand or phrase,
  Or say 'tis not your seal, not your invention;
  You can say none of this. Well, grant it then,
  And tell me in the modesty of honour,
  Why you have given me such clear lights of favour?
  Bade me come smiling and cross-gartered to you,
  To put on yellow stockings, and to frown
  Upon Sir Toby and the lighter people?
  And, acting this in an obedient hope,
  Why have you suffered me to be imprisoned,
340 Kept in a dark house, visited by the priest,
  And made the most notorious geck and gull
  That e'er invention played on? Tell me why?
OLIVIA
  Alas, Malvolio, this is not my writing,
  Though, I confess, much like the character.
  But out of question 'tis Maria's hand.
  And now I do bethink me, it was she
  First told me thou wast mad; then, camest in smiling,
  And in such forms which here were presupposed
  Upon thee in the letter. Prithee, be content.
350 This practice hath most shrewdly passed upon thee;
  But when we know the grounds and authors of it,

Thou shalt be both the plaintiff and the judge
Of thine own cause.
FABIAN   Good madam, hear me speak;
And let no quarrel, nor no brawl to come,
Taint the condition of this present hour,
Which I have wondered at. In hope it shall not,
Most freely I confess, myself and Toby
Set this device against Malvolio here,
Upon some stubborn and uncourteous parts
We had conceived against him. Maria writ   360
The letter at Sir Toby's great importance,
In recompense whereof, he hath married her.
How with a sportful malice it was followed
May rather pluck on laughter than revenge,
If that the injuries be justly weighed
That have on both sides passed.

OLIVIA
Alas, poor fool! How have they baffled thee!

FESTE Why, 'Some are born great, some achieve greatness, and some have greatness thrown upon them.' I
was one, sir, in this interlude, one Sir Topas, sir – but   370
that's all one. 'By the Lord, fool, I am not mad!' But do
you remember: 'Madam, why laugh you at such a
barren rascal, an you smile not, he's gagged'? And thus
the whirligig of time brings in his revenges.

MALVOLIO
I'll be revenged on the whole pack of you!   *Exit*

OLIVIA
He hath been most notoriously abused.

ORSINO
Pursue him and entreat him to a peace.
He hath not told us of the Captain yet.
When that is known, and golden time convents,
A solemn combination shall be made   380

Of our dear souls. Meantime, sweet sister,
We will not part from hence. Cesario, come;
For so you shall be, while you are a man.
But when in other habits you are seen –
Orsino's mistress, and his fancy's queen!

Exeunt all but Feste

FESTE (*sings*)

    When that I was and a little tiny boy,
      With hey-ho, the wind and the rain;
    A foolish thing was but a toy,
      For the rain it raineth every day.

390
    But when I came to man's estate,
      With hey-ho, the wind and the rain;
    'Gainst knaves and thieves men shut their gate,
      For the rain it raineth every day.

    But when I came, alas, to wive,
      With hey-ho, the wind and the rain;
    By swaggering could I never thrive,
      For the rain it raineth every day.

    But when I came unto my beds,
      With hey-ho, the wind and the rain;
    With tosspots still had drunken heads,
      For the rain it raineth every day.

    A great while ago the world began,
      With hey-ho, the wind and the rain;
    But that's all one, our play is done,
      And we'll strive to please you every day.   *Exit*

An Account of the Text

Twelfth Night was first published in the posthumous collection of Shakespeare's plays known as the Folio (1623; abbreviated to F below). It appears there in a very accurate and carefully punctuated text in which misreadings such as *coole my nature* (for *curl by nature*, I.3.94–5) are rare. The play's real puzzles, Mistress Mall's picture and the Lady of the Strachy, are not due to textual corruption but to our ignorance of Elizabethan gossip.

The manuscript of Twelfth Night which was sent to the printer in 1623 was either the copy of the play actually used for productions, known as the prompt book, or a copy of this specially made for the printer. This is evident from the theatrical practicality of the text as it stands. Actors' entrances are given at the point where they must begin to move on to the stage. For example, at V.1.186 Sir Toby starts to struggle in, supported by Feste. Sir Andrew speaks a sentence before he becomes aware of Sir Toby's arrival, and it takes another two lines spoken by Sir Andrew for Sir Toby to get well downstage where Orsino can address him. So, too, the actor playing Malvolio is warned to get ready for the 'dark house' dialogue by the stage direction *Maluolio within*. Exits are not given when it is perfectly plain to the actor that he has to get off the stage. Thus Maria is kept flitting to and fro on errands, but the list of variant stage directions given below shows that most of her exits go unnoted. Nor does Malvolio need any direction to stalk out at *I'll be revenged on the whole pack of you!* (V.1.375), for it is evident from Orsino's next speech that he has done so.

An author's own 'fair copy' could be used as the prompt book in an Elizabethan theatre. Unfortunately there appears to be no evidence that this was the case with *Twelfth Night*. A small piece of evidence that the prompt book was not Shakespeare's fair copy is afforded by the occurrence of *Uiolenta* for *Viola* at I.5.160, *Marian* for *Maria* at II.3.13 and (unless a joke is intended) *Agueface* for *Aguecheek* at I.3.40. Such uncertainty about names is natural in the first act or so of an autograph play, especially one that has been written in haste, but it is likely to be eliminated when the author copies out his work for himself. It is reasonably safe to assume that the manuscript of *Twelfth Night* which reached the playhouse presented the play in a finished form but was not tidy enough to be used as the prompt book, so that a copy had to be made. The possibility that Maria's letter is a stage closer to Shakespeare's autograph manuscript than is the rest of the play is briefly discussed in the Commentary, in notes on II.5.140 and III.4.71.

The act and scene divisions of the Folio are unlikely to be Shakespeare's own. They are quite arbitrary, and the action of the play is in fact continuous between Acts I and II, and between Acts III and IV. Possibly the act divisions were introduced to give an opportunity for intermission music at court performances, such as those in 1618 and 1623. In addition to these act and scene divisions, which are in Latin, F has *Finis Actus primus* (*secundus*, *Quartus*) at the end of Acts I, II and IV.

The variants listed below do not include the few lines printed as prose in the Folio and as verse in this edition (for example, the 'Jolly Robin' song in IV.2) or the few others, such as III.4.19–22, which were erroneously printed in F as verse but are here restored to prose. Following the practice of the Folio, a number of short verse lines have been printed on their own, instead of being shown as halves of lines divided between two speakers, the normal practice of eighteenth- and nineteenth-century editions. Metrical continuity is natural only when one character is responding fully to another, either in affection or anger. When a character follows his or her own thoughts independently of the other speaker (as Viola does in I.2), or when a marked pause or sudden change of mood occurs, Shakespeare does not hesitate to use half-lines, and this edition has tried to preserve his free handling of his poetic medium. On the same principle, no attempt has been made to regularize lines such as *That — methought — her eyes had lost her tongue* (II.2.20). The slight pause before and after the parenthesis lengthens out the line to a normal blank verse, and similar irregularities in other lines can usually be justified in the same way.

It will be seen from the short list of variants below that this is a very conservative text, preserving the Folio readings wherever they make sense. But what is sense in the study is not always sense on the modern stage. The second list is therefore of emendations which producers may wish to adopt in the theatre for the sake of lucidity.

COLLATIONS

1 Emendations

The following is a list of readings in the present text which are departures from the Folio text of 1623. The reading on the right of the square bracket is that of F.

Title   TWELFTH] Twelfe
I.I
        11 sea, naught] Sea. Nought
I.2
        15 Arion] *Orion*
I.3
        26 all, most] almost
        49 SIR ANDREW] *Ma.*
    94–5 curl by nature] coole my nature
     128 dun-coloured] dam'd colour'd
          set] sit
     131 That's] That
I.5
        86 guiltless] guitlesse
      142 He's] Ha's

160 *Viola*] *Uiolenta*

II.2

  31 our frailty] O frailtie

II.3

  2 *diluculo*] *Deliculo*
  24 leman] Lemon
  25 impetticoat] impeticos
  83 O' the twelfth] O the twelfe
 130 a nayword] an ayword
 142 swathes] swarths

II.5

 112 staniel] stallion
 140 *born*] become
 141 *achieve*] atcheeues
 154 champain] champian
 169 *dear*] deero

III.1

  8 king] Kings
 66 wise men, folly-fallen] wisemens folly falne
 88 all ready] already

III.2

  7 see thee the] see the
 50 thy] the
 63 nine] mine
 66 renegado] Renegatho

III.4

 23 OLIVIA] *Mal.*
 71 tang] langer
 289 oath's sake] oath sake

IV.2

  7 student] Studient
 14 Gorboduc] Gorbodacke
 37 clerestories] cleere stores
 51 haply] happily

IV.3

 27 jealous] jealious

V.1

 173 He's] H'as
    he's] has

193 he's] has
197 pavin] panyn

2 *Rejected Emendations*

The following is a list of well-founded emendations which
have not been adopted in this edition. The emendation is in
each case to the right of the square bracket.

I.I
     5 sound] south
   27 heat] hence
I.2
  40–41 sight | And company] company | And sight
I.3
   38 *vulgo*] *volto*
 128 dun-coloured] flame-coloured
I.4
   33 shrill and sound] shrill of sound
I.5
 191 not mad] but mad
197–8 Tell me your mind; I am a messenger] OLIVIA
     Tell me your mind. VIOLA I am a messenger
II.2
  12 of me, I'll nonc] of me! I'll none
  20 That – methought –] That sure methought
  32 made, if such] made of, such
II.3
   9 lives] life
 144 grounds] ground
II.4
  52 Fie away, fie away] Fly away, fly away
  87 It] I
II.5
  33 SIR TOBY] FABIAN
  37 SIR TOBY] FABIAN
169–70 *dear my sweet*] dear, O my sweet
III.2
  50 cubiculo] cubicle

III.3

    15 And thanks. And ever oft] And thanks and ever thanks. And oft

III.4

    88 How is't with you, man?] SIR TOBY How is't with you, man?

    198 unchary on't] unchary out

    203 griefs] grief

    241 computent] competent

    346 lying, vainness] lying vainness

IV.2

  69–70 the upshot] to the upshot

V.1

    112 have] hath

    369 thrown] thrust

3 Stage Directions

There follow the chief departures of this edition from the Folio stage directions. Minor additions such as (*aside*), (*reads*), (*sings*), (*to Feste*), are not noted here.

I.1

    1 *Music*] *not in* F

I.5

    1 *Feste the Clown*] Clowne (*here and elsewhere throughout* F)

    28 *and attendants*] *not in* F

    124 *followed by Maria*] *not in* F

    133 *Exit*] *not in* F

    194 (*showing Viola the way out*)] *not in* F

    210 *Maria and attendants withdraw*] *not in* F

    301 *Exit*] Finis, Actus primus

II.2

    41 *Exit*] *not in* F

II.4

    14 *Exit Curio*] *not in* F

    78 *Curio and attendants withdraw*] *not in* F

II.5

   20 *The men hide. Maria throws down a letter*] *not in F*

   200 *Exeunt*] *Exeunt. Finis Actus secundus*

III.1

   1 *at different entrances . . . playing his pipe and tabor*] *not in F*

   42 *She gives him a coin*] *not in F*

   52 *She gives another coin*] *not in F*

   80 *Maria*] *Gentlewoman*

   90 *Exeunt Sir Toby . . . he, too, leaves*] *not in F*

III.2

   80 *Exeunt*] *Exeunt Omnes*

III.3

   49 *separately*] *not in F*

III.4

   14 *Exit Maria*] *not in F*

   15 *and Maria*] *not in F*

   64 *and Maria different ways*] *not in F*

   196 *Exit Maria. Sir Toby and Fabian stand aside*] *not in F*

   213 *Sir Toby and Fabian come forward*] *Enter Toby and Fabian*

   266 *F gives direction 'Exeunt' for Viola and Fabian*

   282 *(Aside, as he crosses to Fabian)*] *not in F*

   283 *(To Fabian)*] *Enter Fabian and Viola*

   296 *(crossing to Sir Andrew)*] *not in F*

   301 *He draws*] *not in F*

   302 *She draws*] *not in F*

   363 *Exeunt Antonio and Officers*] *Exit*

   375 *Exit*] *not in F*

   384 *Exit*] *not in F*

   386 *Exeunt*] *Exit*

IV.1

   24 *He strikes Sebastian*] *not in F*

   25 *He beats Sir Andrew with the handle of his dagger*] *not in F*

   31 *He grips Sebastian*] *not in F*

   40 *He breaks free and draws his sword*] *not in F*

43 *He draws*] *not in* F
50 *Exeunt Sir Toby, Sir Andrew, and Fabian*] *not in* F

IV.2

3 *Exit*] *not in* F
10 *and Maria*] *not in* F
70 *and Maria*] *not in* F
95, 101 (*In priest's voice*)] *not in* F
99–100, 101 (*In own voice*)] *not in* F

IV.3

35 *Exeunt*] *Exeunt. Finis Actus Quartus*

V.1

140 *Exit an attendant*] *not in* F
205 *Exeunt Sir Toby and Sir Andrew, helped by Feste and
    Fabian*] *not in* F
288 *He reads frantically*] *not in* F
298 (*snatching the letter and giving it to Fabian*)] *not in*
    F
312 *Exit Fabian*] *not in* F
323 *and Fabian*] *not in* F
375 *Exit*] *not in* F
385 *all but Feste*] *not in* F
405 *Exit*] FINIS

The Songs

The editor gratefully acknowledges the assistance of F. W. Sternfeld in the transcribing and editing of the songs.

1. 'O mistress mine' (II.3.37)

No contemporary setting has survived, but there exist two instrumental pieces with this title, both based on the same tune. Their exact relationship to the song in the play is not known, but the tune can be fitted to Shakespeare's words. The words, the tune, or both, may be traditional. The song printed below has been transcribed and edited by Sidney Beck from Thomas Morley's *First Book of Consort Lessons*, published in 1599.

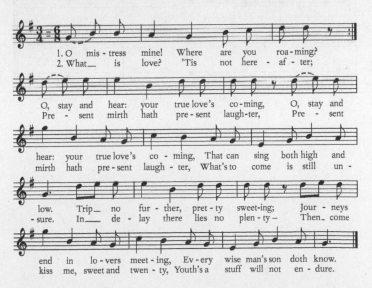

1. O mis-tress mine! Where are you roa-ming?
2. What is love? 'Tis not here - af - ter;

O, stay and hear: your true love's co-ming, O, stay and
Pre - sent mirth hath pre - sent laugh-ter, Pre - sent

hear: your true love's co - ming, That can sing both high and
mirth hath pre - sent laugh - ter, What's to come is still un -

low. Trip no fur - ther, pret - ty sweet-ing; Jour - neys
- sure. In de - lay there lies no plen - ty - Then come

end in lo - vers meet - ing, Ev - ery wise man's son doth know.
kiss me, sweet and twen - ty, Youth's a stuff will not en - dure.

2. 'Hold thy peace' (II.3.67)
This round was published in Thomas Ravenscroft's *Deutero-melia* (1609).

Repeat ad infinitum

3. 'Three merry men' (II.3.75)

The following version of this catch has been transcribed and edited from William Lawes's *Catch That Catch Can* (1652). The tune may go back to Shakespeare's time.

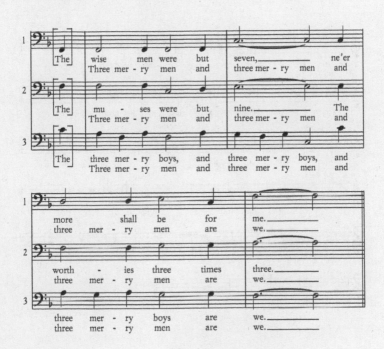

4. 'There dwelt a man in Babylon' (II.3.78)

This is the first line of 'The Ballad of Constant Susanna', which was sung to a corrupt version of 'Greensleeves'.

5. 'O' the twelfth day of December' (II.3.83)

No early music is known.

6. 'Farewell, dear heart' (II.3.99)
This song by Robert Jones was printed in his *First Book of Airs* (1600). It has been transcribed and adapted to the words of the play.

7. 'Come away, come away, death' (II.4.50)
No early music is known.

8. 'Hey Robin' (IV.2.71)

This is part of a round for three or four voices, probably by William Corneyshe (*c.* 1465–*c.* 1523), preserved in the British Museum, Additional MSS. 31922 (sixteenth century; folios 53–4). The full round, transcribed and edited, is given below. It is followed by an arrangement suitable for stage performance.

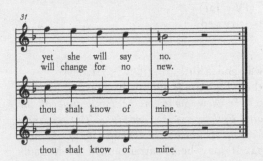

yet   she   will   say   no.
will   change   for   no   new.

thou   shalt   know   of   mine.

thou   shalt   know   of   mine.

MIDDLE PART
(*as sung by* Feste *in a stage production.*)

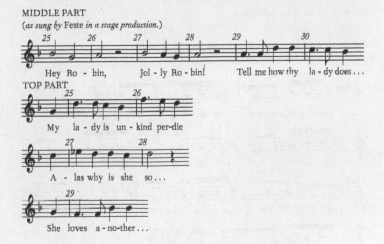

Hey Ro - bin,   Jol - ly Ro - bin!   Tell me how thy   la - dy does . . .

TOP PART

My   la - dy is un - kind per - die

A - las why is she   so . . .

She loves a - no - ther . . .

9. 'I am gone, sir' (IV.2.121)
No early music has survived.

10. 'When that I was and a little tiny boy' (V.1.386)
The tune to which these lines are traditionally sung first appears
in a volume called *The New Songs in the Pantomime of the
Witches; the Celebrated Epilogue in the Comedy of Twelfth Night
. . . sung by Mr Vernon at Vauxhall; composed by J. Vernon*,
and printed in 1772. It may be an arrangement of a traditional melody. The version printed below is based on William
Chappell's *Popular Music of the Olden Time* (1859), where the
source is not identified.

An accompaniment by F. W. Sternfeld is printed in his
Songs from Shakespeare's Tragedies (1964).

Commentary

Folio (F) refers to the first collected edition of Shakespeare's plays, published in 1623. Biblical references are to the Bishops' Bible (1568, etc.), the official English translation of Elizabeth's reign.

The title: The original spelling of the title, *Twelfe Night*, preserves the form of the ordinal number which was common in Shakespeare's day.

I.1

The eighteenth-century custom of localizing scenes ('A street', etc.) has been dropped in this edition. Shakespeare's audience was interested in the relation of characters to one another, not in their relation to any particular place, except when the place itself was part of the action. *Twelfth Night* could have been acted on a very simple stage in a great hall, or perhaps even in the floor space in front of the two big doorways at the screen end of such a hall. These doorways would soon establish themselves as leading to Olivia's house and to Orsino's, and the strangers to the town would arrive by a third entrance, perhaps through the audience. The doors or the curtained doorways could also serve for the box tree and for the dark house or these could be brought on as two substantial properties. The only other requirements would be two or three easily movable seats. No upper stage is needed. When the

play was performed at the Globe, the dark house
could have been represented by the curtained booth
between the two main entrances to the stage.

0 *Music*: At the original production in a great hall,
this music may have been provided by a seated group
of performers on the viol and bass viol, who would
have been playing to the company before the play
started. When the play was repeated in the public
theatre, Orsino's own group of musicians, playing
portable instruments such as recorders, a lute and
an arch-lute, could enter with him.

Orsino: This name may have been suggested by that
of a real duke, Don Virginio Orsino, Duke of Bracciano, who visited Elizabeth I's court in 1600–1601.

3 *appetite*: Orsino's longing for music.

4 *fall*: Cadence.

9–14 *O spirit of love . . . in a minute*: The involved syntax
of these lines perhaps led either the playhouse copyist
or the compositor to insert a full stop after *sea* at
11, but this does not make good sense unless we
read 'Receivest' for *Receiveth*. The general meaning
is clear: love is so ravenous that nothing it devours
can give it real satisfaction.

9 *quick and fresh*: Keen and eager (to devour or consume).

12 *validity*: Value.
   pitch: (1) Height; (2) excellence.

13 *abatement*: Depreciation.

15 *alone*: Exceeding all other passions.
   high fantastical: Intensely imaginative. *fantastical* was
   a fashionable bit of psychological jargon.

19 *Why, so I do*: Orsino's pun on 'heart' and hart' betrays
   his lordly possessiveness; he thinks he should
   command where he adores.

23–4 *And my desires . . . pursue me*: Orsino recalls a classical legend which Shakespeare would know best
   from Ovid's *Metamorphoses* (iii.138 onwards): the
   hunter Actaeon, because he saw the goddess Diana
   naked, was turned into a stag and torn to pieces by
   his hounds. See Introduction.

23 *fell*: Savage.

27 *element*: Sky.

heat: This is often emended to 'hence', but *heat* suggests the way the passage of the seasons will destroy Olivia's beauty, if she spends the best years of her life in mourning.

29 *a cloistress*: An enclosed nun.

31 *eye-offending brine*: Stinging tears.

season: Preserve by salting.

33 *remembrance*: Pronounced as four syllables.

34 *frame*: Construction.

36 *shaft*: Arrow (shot by Cupid).

38 *liver, brain, and heart*: The seats of the passions, judgement and sentiments.

40 *Her sweet perfections*: Olivia's nature will be completed by Orsino's occupying each of these thrones. The condescension is in character, but the idea that 'woman receiveth perfection by the man' is common in the period.

self: Sole.

I.2

o *Viola*: This name probably derives, without Shakespeare being fully aware of the fact, from a romance published in 1598: *The Famous History of Parismus*, by Emanuel Forde. It is set in Thessaly, a country ruled by Queen Olivia. The heroine Violetta disguises herself as a page and seeks service with the man she loves. But apart from this girl-page theme, *Parismus* had little to interest Shakespeare.

2 *Illyria*: This was a region along the eastern coast of the Adriatic, now occupied by Albania, Montenegro and Croatia. See Introduction.

4 *Elysium*: Abode of the happy dead, hence heaven.

6, 7 *perchance*: The Captain and Viola play on the meanings 'perhaps' and 'by good fortune'.

8 *chance*: What may have happened.

11 *driving*: Drifting.

14 *lived*: Kept afloat (a nautical term).

15 *Arion*: This was the name of a Greek musician who

threw himself overboard to escape being murdered by sailors, and was carried to land by a dolphin which had heard him play on the ship. Ovid tells the legend in the *Fasti*, II.79–118.

16 *hold acquaintance with the waves*: 'Bob up and down as if greeting the waves' or perhaps 'follow every movement of the waves'.

19–21 *Mine own escape . . . of him*: My own escape encourages me in the hope, which is warranted by what you have just said, that he also has escaped.

32 *murmur*: Rumour.

43 *delivered*: Revealed.

45 *estate*: Status. Viola does not want her true identity to be disclosed until she has decided the time is ripe for it to be known.

compass: Bring about.

46 *suit*: Petition.

49–50 *nature . . . pollution*: Like the reference to Arion's story in 15, this may be a vestigial remnant of the sea captain's villainy in Rich's 'Apolonius and Silla' (*Elizabethan Love Stories* (1968), ed. T. J. B. Spencer; see Introduction). It also prepares us for Antonio's bitter reproach of what he takes to be Sebastian's treachery later in the play.

52 *character*: Appearance and behaviour.

55–6 *as haply . . . intent*: As may be suitable for the purpose I have shaped.

60 *allow*: Prove.

62 *wit*: Design.

63 *mute*: Dumb attendants, as well as eunuchs, were known by the Elizabethans to be part of the entourage of oriental monarchs.

1.3

1 *my niece*: On the strength of this expression, Sir Toby is usually described as Olivia's uncle. Maria and Olivia herself speak of him as Olivia's 'cousin', but this term could be used in Elizabethan English for any collateral relative other than a brother or sister.

3 *By my troth*: By my faith (an asseveration).

6 *except before excepted*: Exclude what has already been
   excluded (a legal phrase). Sir Toby may mean that
   Olivia has not taken exception to his *ill hours* in
   the past and should not do so now.

8 *modest limits of order*: Bounds of good behaviour.

11 *an*: If.

18 *tall*: Courageous. Maria takes the word in its usual
   sense.
   any's: Any who is.

20 *ducats*: A ducat was worth a third of £1.

21 *have but a year in all these ducats*: Maria means Sir
   Andrew will get through his fortune in a year.

22 *very*: Perfect.

23–4 *viol-de-gamboys*: Bass viol, or viola da gamba
     (ancestor of the modern cello).

25 *without book*: By memory.

26 *natural*: Like an idiot or 'natural'.

28–30 *gift of a coward . . . gift of a grave*: With a play
      on the meanings 'natural ability' and 'present'.

28 *gust*: Relish.

31–2 *substractors*: Detractors.

37 *coistrel*: Groom; low fellow. The word does not occur
   elsewhere in Shakespeare's work, and it has been
   suggested that he picked it up from Barnabe Rich's
   Farewell to Military Profession (1581). But it is not
   uncommon in the period, and still survives in North
   of England dialects.

39 *parish top*: There are several references to parish
   tops in Elizabethan plays, but nothing is known about
   them.
   Castiliano, vulgo: This is a puzzling phrase. We would
   expect it to mean 'Talk of the devil!' (from the
   proverb 'Talk of the devil and he will appear'), since
   Sir Toby has just caught sight of Sir Andrew.
   Castiliano is in fact the name adopted by the devil
   Belphegor when he comes to earth in *Grim the Collier
   of Croydon, or The Devil and his Dame*, a play written
   in or before 1600; and Shakespeare may here be
   alluding to this play in order to give a new twist

to an old saying. He would have been reminded of
the play in reading Rich's collection of tales, because
Rich tells the story on which the play is based —
how the devil was worsted by a woman — in his
Conclusion. Sir Toby's mention of a *parish top* also
connects the two plays. The scene in *Grim the Collier*
which immediately follows Belphegor's assumption
of the name Castiliano starts with Grim complaining,
'Every night I dream I am a town top.' We would
expect *vulgo*, meaning 'in the common tongue', to
be followed by 'devil', but perhaps Sir Toby, warned
by the proverb, makes the gesture of horns instead.
'*Vulgo*' could also follow the noun to which it
referred, and if it does here, Shakespeare, by saying
the devil was Castiliano in the common tongue,
or to the common people, is commenting on the popularity of the other play.

40 *Agueface*: This form of Sir Andrew's name has led
editors to emend *vulgo* to '*volto*' and explain that
Sir Toby is telling Maria to put on a solemn face
like a Castilian, or Spaniard, to suit with Sir
Andrew's expression. Shakespeare is often, however,
a little uncertain about the form of a character's
name near the beginning of a play, and there may
be no joke intended.
Sir Andrew Aguecheek: This name has been learnedly
explained as being from Spanish '*andrajo*', 'a despi-
cable person', or from '*aguicia chica*' meaning 'little
wit'. But to Shakespeare's audience it would simply
suggest the shaking cheeks of cowardice.

44 *shrew*: This is usually explained as an allusion to
Maria's mouse-like size. It could also be another
unconscious recollection of *Grim the Collier*, in which
the devil's human wife is an untamable shrew called
Marian and a waiting-gentlewoman into the bargain.

46 *Accost*: Great play is made with the word '*accostare*'
in *Gl'Ingannati*, but plays contemporary with *Twelfth
Night* show that it was also fashionable in England,
in the form 'accost', at the end of the sixteenth

century. Like *board* (54), it was a nautical metaphor, meaning 'address' or 'greet'. Sir Andrew takes both words in a more concrete sense than Sir Toby intends.

48 *chambermaid*: Not a menial position; more like the modern 'lady companion'.

58 *let part so*: Let her go thus (without ceremony).

62 *in hand*: To deal with.

64 *Marry*: A mild oath, originally 'By Mary'.

66 *Thought is free*: This was the stock retort to 'Do you think I'm a fool?' and is one of many proverbs and stock phrases to do with fools and folly used in this play.

67 *buttery bar*: Ledge in front of the hatch through which drink was handed out from the buttery, or storeroom for liquor.

70 *It's dry*: Maria means 'thirsty', but hints at a supposed sign of impotence. In *Othello*, III.4.38 a moist palm 'argues fruitfulness and liberal heart'.

72 *keep my hand dry*: In allusion to the proverb 'Fools have wit enough to keep themselves dry'.

73 *A dry jest*: Maria puns on the meanings 'stupid' and 'mocking, ironic'.

77 *canary*: A sweet wine, originally from the Canary Islands.

78 *put down*: Defeated in repartee. Sir Andrew plays with the literal meaning.

81 *a Christian*: Any normal man.
   an ordinary man: Since *Christian* here means 'ordinary' in the modern sense, *an ordinary man* may here mean a courtier granted a daily allowance of meals. The ordinary was the common table.

82 *eater of beef*: Medical writers of the period argued that beef made men low and melancholy, and 'beef-witted' is an insult in *Troilus and Cressida*, II.1.12.

87 *Pourquoi*: Why? (French).

94-5 *curl by nature*: F reads *coole my nature*. This skilful emendation by the eighteenth-century editor, Theobald, is confirmed by the pun on *tongues* and 'tongs', which were pronounced alike in Elizabethan

English, and by the antithesis between 'art' and
nature.

98 *huswife*: The F spelling preserves Sir Toby's pun.
'Housewife' (Middle English 'huswif') and 'hussy'
had diverged in meaning but not in pronunciation
at this time. The Elizabethans believed venereal
disease and sexual excess to be among the causes of
baldness.

109 *kickshawses*: Trifles (French '*quelquechoses*').

111 *betters*: Social superiors.

112 *old man*: Old hand; someone experienced.

113 *galliard*: This was a lively five-step dance in which
the fifth step was a leap, or caper. The puns in the
next few lines may owe something to the quibbles
on dancing terms in the epistle dedicatory in Rich's
Farewell to Military Profession.

114 *caper*: Sir Toby quibbles on the meaning 'a spice to
season mutton'.

116 *back-trick*: Sir Andrew means either the special back-
ward leap called the *riccacciata*, or the reversed series
of steps in a galliard; but the audience is meant to
catch the sexual meaning of *trick*, following on
mutton, which could mean 'a loose woman'.

120 *Mistress Mall's picture*: Paintings were frequently
protected by curtains. Mistress Mall has been identified as Mary Fitton, a lady-in-waiting who became
involved in a court scandal in 1601. But there must
have been quite a number of Malls whose pictures
took dust − that is, who lost their good name −
around 1600. If the allusion is literary, it could be
to the sub-plot of John Marston's *Jack Drum's Entertainment* (1600), a play which has some interesting
verbal parallels with *Twelfth Night*.

122 *coranto*: A fast, skipping dance.

123 *sink-apace*: The French '*cinquepas*', or five-step dance,
was very similar to the galliard. There is a quibble
on *sink* meaning 'sewer'. Beatrice quibbles differently with the word in *Much Ado About Nothing*,
II.1.66−71.

126 *the star of a galliard*: A dancing star (another recollection of Beatrice).

128 *dun-coloured stock*: Brown-coloured stocking. From
what is known of Elizabethan handwriting, this is
the most convincing of many emendations suggested
for F's *dam'd colour'd*.

130 *Taurus*: The twelve constellations, of which Taurus,
the Bull, is one, were each held to govern a different
part of the body.

I.4

2 *Cesario*: Viola's assumed name could come from Curio
Gonzaga's comedy, *Gl'Inganni*, published in 1592, in
which the heroine disguises herself as a page and
assumes the name of Cesare. This has been taken as
evidence that when Manningham said *Twelfth Night*
resembled *Gl'Inganni* he meant Gonzaga's play, and not
the earlier anonymous play *Gl'Ingannati*. But there are
very few other resemblances between Shakespeare's
play and Gonzaga's. In the Italian and French tales based
on *Gl'Ingannati* which Shakespeare certainly did read,
the heroine calls herself Romulo or Romule because she
is from Rome, and in making Viola call herself Cesario,
which has the same associations, Shakespeare may be
echoing these narrative versions.

5 *his humour*: The changefulness of his disposition.

6–7 *Is he . . . favours*: Asked with anxiety.

15 *address thy gait*: Direct your steps.

16 *access*: This is accented on the second syllable.

28 *nuncio*: Messenger.
aspect: This is accented on the second syllable.

32 *rubious*: Ruby-red.
pipe: Voice.

33 *sound*: Unbroken.

34 *semblative*: Like; resembling.
part: A theatrical term; Shakespeare is thinking of
his company's boy actors.

35 *constellation*: Character (as decided by the stars).

39–40 *And thou shalt live . . . thine*: Orsino speaks more
truly than he knows.

41 *barful strife*: Struggle to overcome my disinclination (to woo on Orsino's behalf).

1.5

0 *Feste*: *Clowne* in all speech-prefixes of the Folio text. The name suggests a feast or festivity.

3 *hang thee*: An exaggeration, like 'You'll be shot'.

5 *fear no colours*: In using this catchphrase for 'fear nothing' Feste puns on 'colours' and 'collars'. Maria in her reply reverts to the original meaning of 'colours' in this phrase – 'military standards'.

6 *Make that good*: Explain that.

8 *good lenten answer*: Thin joke.

13–14 *Well, God give them . . . talents*: Feste's special line in jesting is a mock sanctimoniousness, which often gives his speech a biblical flavour. Here there are echoes of 'For unto him that hath, shall it be given' (Mark 4:25) and of the parable of the good steward who put out his talent to usury. Feste implies that his seeming foolishness is a God-given insight.

16 *turned away*: Dismissed.

19 *let summer bear it out*: May the fine weather hold! In the same way the dismissed Fool in *Two Maids of More-clacke* (printed 1608, acted earlier), a part played by Robert Armin, says, 'The summer's day is long, the winter's nights be short.'

21 *points*: Maria seizes on the meaning 'laces to hold up breeches', perhaps with a pun on '*resolvo*' (Latin), 'untie'.

23 *gaskins*: Loose breeches.

24–6 *if Sir Toby . . . Illyria*: This gives a hint of the marriage which is to occur before the end of the play.

28 *you were best*: It would be best for you.

Malvolio: It is just, but only just, conceivable that this name was suggested to Shakespeare by the name of Messer Agnol Malevolti, a lovesick character in the Italian play *Il Sacrificio*, which was acted as a form of curtain-raiser to *Gl'Ingannati*. Shakespeare could have made up this name suggestive of churlishness and misplaced desire, himself – influenced maybe by the expression '*mala volgia*' which occurs several times in Bandello's Italian version of the tale. But cf. 'Benvolio' in *Romeo and Juliet*.

29 *Wit*: Intelligence.

32 *Quinapalus*: Feste takes off the pedantry of quoting obscure authorities. This no longer gets a laugh, and the actor may be grateful for Leslie Hotson's suggestion that Feste here pretends to consult the carved head on his fool's stick, or bauble – even if he cannot accept the explanation that '*quinapalo*' is an italianate nonce-word for 'there on a stick'.

36 *Go to*: An expression of impatience, like our 'Come, come'.

dry: Barren (of jests).

37 *dishonest*: Unreliable.

40–42 *mend*: Feste plays with the meanings 'repair' and 'reform'.

42 *botcher*: Tailor who does repairs.

45 *simple syllogism*: In this quibbling parody of formal deductive reasoning, Feste reminds Olivia that she must not expect too much of her fool, who is a mixture of vices and virtues like the rest of humanity; he then moves easily on to the suggestion that she should not expect her own grief to be unnaturally prolonged.

46 *no true cuckold but calamity*: Olivia seems, like Juliet, to be 'wedded to calamity'; but no one can mourn for ever – nor should Olivia try to do so, since while she tries her beauty will fade. There is probably a pun on *cuckold* and 'cockle', meaning 'weed'.

50 *Misprision*: Wrongful arrest (with a play on the more common meaning of 'misunderstanding').

50–51 *cucullus non facit monachum*: The cowl does not make the monk (Latin proverb).

55 *Dexteriously*: A common Elizabethan variant of 'dexterously'.

57–8 *Good my mouse of virtue*: Assuming his Sir Topas

voice, Feste speaks to Olivia as a priest catechizing
a small girl.

59 *idleness*: Pastime.
   bide: abide; wait for.

69 *mend*: Improve.

71–2 *Infirmity . . . the better fool*: The bitterness of Malvolio's
reply is due to his realization that Olivia has forgiven
Feste, and is not going to turn him away.

75 *no fox*: Not cunning. By emphasizing *I*, Feste shows
he is aware of Malvolio's scheming.

79 *put down*: Defeated in repartee.

80 *ordinary fool . . . stone*: If this is a reference to
Stone the Fool, a well-known Elizabethan jester,
ordinary means 'of a tavern or eating-house'. Stone
is called a tavern fool in Ben Jonson's *Volpone*,
II.1.53–4.

81 *he's out of his guard*: He has used up all his retorts
(a fencing metaphor).

82 *minister occasion*: Supply opportunity.

83 *set*: Not spontaneous.

84 *zanies*: These were the professional fools' stooges
who fed them with matter for jests and unsuccessfully imitated their tricks. Olivia naturally resents
this description of her father and herself.

87 *free*: Magnanimous. Like 'generous', the word
suggests good breeding.

87–8 *bird-bolts*: Short, blunt arrows.

89 *allowed*: Licensed.

90 *known discreet man*: Olivia, regaining her equanimity,
tactfully turns her reproach into a compliment.

92 *Mercury endue thee with leasing*: May the god of decep-
tion make you a good liar.

98 *well attended*: With several attendants.

108 *Jove*: Here and elsewhere this is almost certainly a
substitution for 'God' in the play's original text, and
must have been made after 27 May 1606, when a
statute was passed against stage profanity.

110 *pia mater*: Brain (actually the membrane covering
the brain).

115 *here*: F's *heere* may represent a stage direction which
indicated a hiccup or belch.

116 *sot*: Fool.

123 *an*: If.

124 *faith*: Strengthened more by faith than works, Sir
Toby lurches out to defy the devil.
followed by Maria: Maria's exit is not marked in F.
The producer may prefer to make her leave later
with Feste.

127 *above heat*: Above a normal temperature. Drink was
thought to heat the blood.

129 *crowner*: Coroner.

143 *sheriff's post*: A post was set up to mark the house
of the civic authority. The custom persists in
Scotland.

146 *of mankind*: Fierce. Leontes calls Paulina 'A mankind
witch' in *The Winter's Tale*, II.3.67.

148–9 *will you or no*: Whether or not you are willing.

150 *personage*: Appearance.

152 *a squash*: An unripe peascod.

153 *a codling*: An unripe apple.

153–4 *in standing water*: At the turn of the tide.

154–5 *well-favoured*: Handsome.

155 *shrewishly*: Sharply and like a woman.

167 *con*: Learn by heart.

168–9 *comptible . . . usage*: Sensitive to even the least slight.

173 *modest assurance*: Just enough assurance to satisfy me.

175 *a comedian*: An actor.

176–7 *my profound heart . . . fangs of malice*: Viola acknowledges Olivia's penetration, but protests at her mali-
ciousness.

179 *usurp*: Counterfeit. Viola takes the word in a more
literal sense, as meaning 'to exercise a power which
is not yours by right'.

182 *from my commission*: Not part of my instructions.

185 *forgive*: Excuse (from delivering).

188 *feigned*: This may be an echo of *As You Like It*,
where Touchstone maintains (III.3.17–18) that 'the
truest poetry is the most feigning'.

190–91 *If you be not mad . . . if you have reason*: The antithesis here is between partial sanity and complete sanity, or reason. There is no need to emend.

192 *'Tis not that time of moon with me*: I am not sufficiently lunatic.

196 *swabber*: Deckhand. Viola retorts in Maria's own nautical language.
hull: Drift with furled sails.

197 *Some mollification for*: Pray pacify.
giant: Used ironically of Maria.

197–8 *Tell me your mind*: Nearly all editors give this to Olivia. But Viola thinks she is on the point of being dismissed, and wants at least to be able to take back a message to Orsino. Olivia, however, is becoming increasingly interested in Viola, and asks her to deliver whatever message she has been entrusted with. This emboldens Viola to ask that all bystanders should be sent out of earshot.

200 *courtesy*: Preliminary greetings (said ironically, either of Viola's behaviour at the gate or of a scuffle at the door with Maria).
fearful: Alarming.
Speak your office: Tell me what you have been entrusted with.

201 *It alone concerns your ear*: It is meant to be heard only by you.

202 *taxation of homage*: Demand for money to be paid as an acknowledgement of vassalage.

207 *entertainment*: Reception.

208–9 *divinity . . . profanation*: The language of the religion of love.

213 *comfortable*: Comforting.

217 *by the method*: In the same style.

222 *are now out of your text*: Have changed the subject.

224 *such a one I was this present*: This is a recent portrait of me. Olivia throws back her veil as if she were revealing a curtained picture of herself.

227 *'Tis in grain*: The colour is fast.

228 *blent*: Blended. Viola keeps up the image of a painting.

229 *cunning*: Skilful.

232 *copy*: Viola means a child, but Olivia pounces on the literal meaning.

234 *divers schedules*: Various lists.

235 *labelled*: Attached as a codicil.

236 *indifferent*: Fairly.

238 *praise*: Appraise; estimate.

243 *The nonpareil of beauty*: The one unmatched in beauty.

244 *fertile*: Copious.

249 *In voices well divulged*: Well spoken of.
free: Well bred. Orsino has the courtier's, scholar's and soldier's qualities, and so represents, like Hamlet, the Renaissance ideal.

251 *A gracious person*: Endowed with a good physique.

257 *willow*: Associated with rejected love, as in the willow song in *Othello*.

258 *my soul*: Olivia.

259 *cantons*: Songs (from Italian 'canzone', by confusion with 'canto' from Latin 'cantus').

261 *Hallow*: The F spelling for 'halloo' is kept, because it conveys also the idea of 'bless'.

262 *babbling gossip*: Echo personified.

265 *But*: Unless.

267 *state*: Social standing.

273 *fee'd post*: Messenger to be tipped.

275 *Love make*: May the god of love make.
that you shall love: (The man) whom you will love.

282 *blazon*: A coat of arms. Cesario's bearing declares his high birth.

285 *perfections*: Pronounced as four syllables.

291 *County*: This was a common Elizabethan form of 'count', keeping the two syllables of the Old French 'contë'.

292 *Would I or not*: Whether I wanted it or not.

293 *flatter with*: Encourage.

299 *Mine eye . . . my mind*: My eye will betray my reason into thinking too well of him (Cesario).

300 *owe*: Own; control.

II.1

1–2 *will you not that I go*: Do you not want me to go.

3 *By your patience*: If you will be so forbearing.

4 *malignancy*: Evil influence (an astrological term).

5 *distemper*: Disorder; disturb.

9 *sooth*: Indeed.

9–10 *my determinate voyage is mere extravagancy*: I only intend to wander.

12–13 *it charges me . . . myself*: Courtesy obliges me all the more to reveal who I am.

15 *Messaline*: This is probably the modern Marseilles. The inhabitants of Marseilles and of Illyria are mentioned together ('*Massiliensis, Hilurios*') in a speech about one twin looking for another twin in Plautus' *Menaechmi*, l. 235. Shakespeare could also have had the word suggested to him by the occurrence of Messilina as a name in the story preceding 'Apolonius and Silla' in Rich's *Farewell to Military Profession*.

17 *in an hour*: At the same time.

20 *breach*: Surf; breakers.

24 *estimable*: Appreciative. Sebastian means that he could not, in modesty, go so far as to marvel at the beauty of his twin sister.

25 *publish*: Speak openly of.

28 *with more*: With more salt water (that is, with tears).

29 *entertainment*: Treatment as my guest.

31 *murder me for my love*: Cause me to die of grief at leaving you. Sebastian's reply is just as exaggerated: he would rather die than let Antonio demean himself by waiting on him.

34 *desire*: Request.

35 *kindness*: Tender feelings.

37 *tell tales of me*: Betray my feelings (by tears).

II.2

0 *several doors*: Separate entrances. The doors are those leading on to the stage or acting area; the scene itself is unlocalized.

1 *even*: Just.

4 *arrived but hither*: Come only this far.

8 *desperate assurance*: Certainty beyond all hope.

  she will none of him: She wants nothing to do with him.

12 *She took the ring of me*: A quick-witted lie to conceal Olivia's indiscretion from her steward.

  of me: From me.

15 *in your eye*: Where you can see it.

18 *charmed*: Cast a spell over.

19 *made good view of me*: Examined me closely.

20 *lost*: Lost touch with; failed to coordinate with.

22 *cunning*: Craftiness.

28 *the pregnant enemy*: Satan.

  pregnant: Wily.

29 *proper false*: Handsome deceivers.

31–2 *Alas, our frailty is the cause, not we,* | *For such as we are made, if such we be*: These lines continue the idea of something being formed or made, like a wax seal: 'Alas, women's frailty is the cause, not women themselves, for what happens to us – if we are like that.' The lines make reasonable sense, but are not easy to get across in a theatre, and producers may prefer the emendation accepted by many editors: *Alas, our frailty is the cause, not we!* | *For such as we are made of, such we be.*

33 *fadge*: Turn out.

34 *monster*: Neither man nor woman.

  fond: Dote.

39 *thriftless*: Wasted; useless.

II.3

2 *betimes*: Early.

  diluculo surgere: The adage '*dīlūculo sūrgere salūberrimum est*' ('to get up at dawn is most healthy') occurs in *Lily's Grammar*, a popular sixteenth-century schoolbook.

4 *troth*: Faith.

9 *four elements*: The basic components of the world – fire, air, water, earth.

13 *stoup*: Two-pint jug (pronounced 'stoop').

16 *We Three*: Trick pictures, or anamorphoses, with this

title were common at the time. One such picture
shows a fool's head if viewed the right way up and
another fool's head if viewed upside down. The
spectator who asked 'Where's the third?' would be
invited to view the picture from the side, where it
took on the form of a donkey, and would then be
asked (in Bottom's words) 'You see an ass head of
your own, do you?' Hence Sir Toby's retort of
Welcome, ass!

17 *catch*: Round (a song with a continuous melody that
could be divided into parts, each harmonizing with
the others).

18 *breast*: Singing voice.

19 *leg*: The bow with which Feste begins and ends his
songs.

21 *gracious*: Talented; inspired.

22-3 *Pigrogromitus . . . Queubus*: Feste's astronomical
patter is mock-learning of the kind he later displays
as Sir Topas. The names are probably Shakespeare's
invention.

24 *leman*: Sweetheart.

25 *impetticoat*: (For F's *impeticos*) pocket (in reference
to the fool's long coat; a nonce-word).
gratillity: Little tip (another nonce-word, probably
a diminutive formed from 'gratuity').

25-7 *Malvolio's nose is no whipstock, my lady has a white
hand, and the Myrmidons are no bottle-ale houses*: No
explanation satisfactorily connects these three statements. If *whipstock* means a wooden post or handle,
Feste is saying Malvolio's nose is sensitive enough
to smell out Sir Andrew's tip. If it means 'the piece
of wood attached to a ship's tiller', he is saying
much the same thing – that Malvolio can't be led
by the nose. One attractive suggestion is that
Malvolio, by reason of his haughty hooked nose (not
straight like a whipstock), seems destined for greatness, and Olivia is ripe for marriage, a meaning of
'white hand' found in several Shakespeare plays; but
the conclusion, that Malvolio is an upstart who as

a Count will abolish cakes and ale, is less convincing.
my lady could be Feste's leman, who likes to be
taken to the most expensive inns such as the
Myrmidons (perhaps with a pun on 'Mermaidens').

32 *testril*: Sixpence (a variant of 'teston', a silver coin).

33 *give a —*: As there is no point here in an interrup-
tion, it appears that a line was passed over by the
compositor.

34 *a song of good life*: A drinking song. But Sir Andrew
takes it to be a moral song or hymn.

37 *O mistress mine*: Two instrumental versions of a tune
with this title are known: one for a small band, by
Thomas Morley, was published in 1599 and the other,
for keyboard, by William Byrd, was published in 1619.
A modern transcription of Morley's air is given in
The Songs. Both pieces may be based on a popular
Elizabethan tune to which the comic actor, playwright and singer Robert Armin (*c.* 1568–1615), who
joined Shakespeare's company in the late 1590s, also
sang Shakespeare's lyric. But we cannot be sure that
Shakespeare intended to use this tune, which also
occurs in an early-seventeenth-century commonplace
book as the setting for a quite different lyric.

40 *sweeting*: Darling.

42 *Every wise man's son*: In allusion to the saying that
wise men have fools for their sons.

52 *contagious*: Sir Toby means 'catchy', but Sir Andrew's
sweet and contagious sounds so odd, in view of the
usual meaning of 'contagious' – 'infectious; evil-
smelling' – that Sir Toby goes on to echo Sir Andrew
(*dulcet in contagion*) and say that a phrase like this
could be used only if we heard with our noses.
Shakespeare may have remembered an equally forced
use of 'contagious' in 'Apolonius and Silla': 'But
Silla, the further that she saw herself bereaved of
all hope ever any more to see her beloved Apolonius,
so much the more contagious were her passions . . .'
(*Elizabethan Love Stories* (1968), ed. T. J. B. Spencer).

55 *welkin*: Sky.

56–7 *three souls out of one weaver*: Sir Toby boasts that
their catch will not only make the sky dance, but
will have three times the usual effect of music on
a pious weaver. Weavers were often Calvinist
refugees from the Low Countries, who would be in
ecstasy on hearing a well-sung psalm; and someone
in an ecstasy appears to be without movement, feeling
or thought, and so without the three souls – of
motion, feeling and sense – which man was held to
possess by the medieval philosophers.

58 *An*: If.
dog at: Clever at.

63 *Hold thy peace*: A tune for this round is given in
The Songs. The effect when it is sung is that of a
brawl, with each singer calling the others 'knave'.

73 *Cataian*: Chinese. Olivia is inscrutable.
politicians: Schemers.

74 *Peg-a-Ramsey*: A ballad about a jealous, spying wife
was sung to this popular Elizabethan dance tune, so
Sir Toby, if he is not so drunk that he is talking
nonsense, may mean that Malvolio is keeping a
watchful eye on the *politicians*.

75 *Three merry men*: We have the words but not the music
of several Elizabethan songs ending with this phrase.
The music given in The Songs is that of a round
in a collection made by the early-seventeenth-century
composer William Lawes, of which the final line
was originally: 'And three merry boys, and three
merry boys, and three merry boys are we.'

77 *Tilly-vally*: It has been suggested that this is another
snatch of song, as a tune has been found with
the title 'Tilly-vally, any money'. But it is more
probably an exclamation of impatience on Sir Toby's
part.

78 *There dwelt a man in Babylon*: In mocking Maria's
use of *lady*, Sir Toby recalls a ballad about Susanna
and the Elders which has this word for its refrain.
The first stanza is quoted in Percy's *Reliques of
Ancient English Poetry*, ii. x:

> There dwelt a man in Babylon
>   Of reputation great by fame;
> He took to wife a fair woman,
>   Susanna she was called by name:
> A woman fair and virtuous;
>   Lady, lady:
> Why should we not of her learn thus
>   To live godly?

79 *Beshrew me*: Curse me.

81–2 *grace . . . natural*: By making use of the theolog-
ical distinction between grace and nature, Sir Andrew
inadvertently calls himself a *natural* fool.

83 *O' the twelfth day of December*: No song beginning
with these words is known. Sir Toby may be
misquoting the ballad of 'Musselburgh Field', which
starts 'On the tenth day of December'. Or his words
could be a misquotation of the first line of the carol
called 'The Twelve Days of Christmas', which traditionally begins 'On the twelfth day . . .' and not as
it is usually sung nowadays 'On the first day . . .'

86 *wit*: Sense.

honesty: Decency.

87 *tinkers*: These were noted for their songs and their
drinking. In *Egregious Popish Impostures* (1603), Richard
Harsnet writes about a 'master setter of catches or
rounds, used to be sung by tinkers as they sit by the fire
with a pot of good ale between their legs'.

89 *coziers*: Cobblers (who also sang at their work).

89–90 *mitigation or remorse of voice*: Lowering your voices
out of consideration.

92 *Sneck up*: Originally meaning 'Go and be hanged',
this survives in both American and British dialects
with the meaning 'Make yourself scarce!'.

93 *round*: Blunt.

99 *Farewell, dear heart*: Sir Toby and Feste sing their
own version of a song which is given in Robert
Jones's *First Book of Airs* (1600). See The Songs.

104 *there you lie*: Probably Sir Toby has fallen over.

110 *Out o'tune*: A way of refuting Feste's denial and taking his 'dare'.

112 *cakes and ale*: These were traditional at Church feasts, and so repugnant to Puritans, who would also be offended at the mention of St Anne, mother of the Virgin Mary.

113 *ginger*: This was a favourite Elizabethan spice, and the sheep-shearing feast in *The Winter's Tale* calls for a root or two of ginger. Robert Armin liked ginger washed down with ale.

116 *chain*: Chain of office. There is a reference to this method of cleaning such insignia in Webster's *The Duchess of Malfi*, III.2. Sir Toby is reminding Malvolio of his station in Olivia's household.

121 *shake your ears*: A contemptuous dismissal, equivalent to calling Malvolio a donkey.

123 *challenge him the field*: Challenge him to a duel. The suggestion shows Sir Andrew's ill breeding, as it was a social solecism to challenge an inferior.

130 *gull*: Trick.
    nayword: Byword.

131 *common recreation*: Source of amusement for everyone.

133 *Possess us*: Give us the facts.

136 *exquisite*: A difficult word for the drunken knights to get their tongues round. Shakespeare puts it twice in the mouth of Cassio, to mark his increasing drunkenness, in *Othello*, II.3.18, 93.

141 *time-pleaser*: Time-server.
    affectioned: Affected.

141–2 *cons state without book*: Learns high-sounding phrases by heart.

142 *swathes*: A swathe is the grass cut at a single sweep of a scythe. The image is of a huge circuitous period falling like hay about the listener's ears.

142–3 *the best persuaded of himself*: Thinking better of himself than anyone else does.

150 *expressure*: Expression.

152 *feelingly personated*: Vividly described.

163 *Ass*: Maria puns on 'as' and 'ass'.

165 *physic*: Medicine (to purge Malvolio's conceit).

166–7 *let the fool make a third*: It is odd that Feste himself says nothing in this part of the scene. Producers have sometimes made him exit in the wake of Malvolio, or even fall asleep until the end of the scene.

168 *construction*: Interpretation.

170 *Penthesilea*: An Amazonian queen. Maria's spirit is out of all proportion to her size.

172 *beagle*: A small but keen and intelligent hound.

177 *recover*: Get hold of.

178 *out*: Out of pocket.

180 *cut*: A term of contempt, in reference to a cut horse, or gelding.

183 *burn some sack*: Warm and spice some Spanish wine.

II.4

1 *good morrow*: Good morning.

2 *good Cesario*: It has been suggested that Shakespeare altered this scene to make Feste the singer, and that this opening indicates his original intention of having Viola sing the song. But Orsino may simply be inviting Viola to listen to the song with him. See Introduction.

3 *antique*: Strange and old-world.

5 *recollected terms*: Studied phrases. New-fangled words accompanied new-fangled music: *airs* were all the rage around 1601.

18 *Unstaid*: Unsteady.
   motions: Emotions.

21–2 *It gives a . . . throned*: It awakens an immediate response in the heart.

22 *masterly*: From experience, as one who has mastered the art of love.

24 *favour*: Face.

25 *by your favour*: A slight stress on *your* shows that Viola is playing with the meanings 'if you please' and 'like you in feature'.

29 *still*: Always.

30 *wears she*: She adapts herself.

31 *sways she level in her husband's heart*: Her husband's love for her remains steady.

34 *worn*: Exhausted. Orsino seems inconstant even to his belief in his own constancy.

35 *I think it well*: Viola says this hesitantly and with mixed feelings, since she both wants and does not want Orsino to be inconstant. The plot unties this particular knot for her.

37 *hold the bent*: Remain at full stretch (a metaphor from archery).

39 *displayed*: Unfolded; opened (not merely 'shown').

44 *spinsters*: Spinners.

45 *free*: This can mean either 'unattached' or 'free from care'. To Orsino these are one and the same thing. *weave their thread with bones*: Make lace on bone bobbins.

46 *silly sooth*: Simple truth.

47 *dallies with*: Dwells on.

48 *the old age*: The good old days.

50 *Come away, come away, death*: No contemporary setting of this has been discovered.

51 *cypress*: This could be either a coffin of cypress wood or a bier decorated with boughs of cypress. There are references to both in the period.

52 *Fie away*: Be off!

56-7 *My part . . . share it*: No one so faithful has ever received his allotted portion, death.

60 *greet*: Bewail. This verb was no longer used transitively in the sixteenth century, but perhaps this is one of the things that give Feste's song its antique flavour.

67 *No pains, sir*: Feste seems to resent Orsino's offhand payment.

69 *pleasure will be paid*: Proverbial.

71 *leave, to leave thee*: A courteous dismissal.

72 *the melancholy god*: Saturn, whose planet ruled those of a melancholy humour.

73 *changeable*: Shot (having the weft of one colour and the woof of another so that the material shows

different colours when viewed from different angles).

74 *opal*: Semi-precious stone which changes colour with changes in the light.

74–7 *I would . . . nothing*: The captain of a merchant ship with no fixed schedule would be able to pick up cargoes easily.

80 *the world*: Society.

82 *parts*: Gifts of wealth and position.

83 *giddily*: Lightly; carelessly. Fortune was a fickle goddess.

84 *that miracle*: Her beauty.

85 *pranks*: Adorns.

87 *Sooth*: In truth.

93 *bide*: Bear.

95–8 *retention . . . cloyment, and revolt*: *retention* is a medical term meaning 'the power to retain'. Orsino is not speaking metaphorically; in Shakespeare's day, the emotions were held to have physiological origins. Thus the liver (generative of the digestive juices) is not only to the appetite as real passion is to a passing fancy, but is itself the seat of the passions. See also I.1.38–9.

111 *damask*: The contrast with *green and yellow melancholy*, suggesting the unhealthy pallor of grief, shows that the mingled pink and white of the damask rose is meant here.

113 *Patience on a monument*: Both here and in *Pericles* V.1.137–8 – 'Like Patience gazing on kings' graves, and smiling | Extremity out of act' – Shakespeare has in mind some such allegorical figure as the representation of Patience in *Iconologia* (1593), a popular Elizabethan reference book, where she is seated on a stone with a yoke on her shoulders and her feet on thorns.

116 *Our shows are more than will*: We display more passion than we actually feel.

120 *And all the brothers too*: Viola remembers Sebastian with these words, and the thought deepens the scene's melancholy.

123 *denay*: Denial.

II.5

    0 *Fabian*: This name may echo 'Fabio', the girl-page's assumed name in *Gl'Ingannati*. Fabian's position in Olivia's household seems to be that of a hanger-on, rather than of a paid servant.

    3 *boiled to death*: A piece of facetiousness; melancholy was a cold humour.

    5 *sheep-biter*: Originally a dog that attacks sheep; so a slang word meaning a sneaking fellow.

    8 *bear-baiting*: This explanation of Fabian's presence fits in with the mention of Malvolio as a kind of Puritan; the Puritans were fiercely opposed to bear-baiting.

    12 *An*: If.

    14 *metal of India*: Pure gold (with a pun on 'mettle').

    19 *a contemplative idiot*: The kind of imbecile who gazes into vacuity.

    Close: Hide.

    22 *tickling*: Flattery. Trout can be caught in shallow pools by rubbing them round the gills.

    24 *affect*: Care for.

    26 *complexion*: Temperament.

    31 *jets*: Struts.

    32 *'Slight*: An oath – 'by God's light'.

    38–9 *The lady of the Strachy married the yeoman of the wardrobe*: One explanation of this is that William Strachy was a shareholder in the Children's company at Blackfriars Theatre early in the seventeenth century, and either he or his wife visited the theatre two or three times a week to collect their share of the takings in the presence of David Yeomans, tiresman (wardrobe-keeper) of the company, whom Strachy's widow can be presumed eventually to have married. But if the allusion is in fact to these people, it must have been added to the play a very little time before it was printed in F, as William Strachy did not die till 1621. The two definite articles make it hard to accept this statement as an allusion to Strachy's wife and David Yeomans. 'Yeoman of a wardrobe' was a generic name for a tiresman, but *the* Wardrobe usually meant the Queen's Wardrobe in the Blackfriars precinct – as it does in Shakespeare's will. *The* Strachy sounds like the name of a house rather than a man. Probably the allusion is to a piece of Blackfriars or court gossip of 1601 or 1602 which is not recorded elsewhere.

40 *Jezebel*: The shameless wife of King Ahab; see 1 Kings 16:31 onwards.

42 *blows him*: Puffs him up.

44 *state*: Canopied chair of state.

45 *stone-bow*: Crossbow from which small stones could be shot.

46–7 *branched velvet*: Velvet brocade.

51 *to have the humour of state*: To be up on my dignity.

52 *demure travel of regard*: Grave look round the company.

58 *make out*: Go out.

59 *with my –*: Malvolio is fingering his steward's chain of office when he suddenly realizes he will no longer be wearing it; see Introduction.

61 *curtsies*: Bows low.

63–4 *Though our silence . . . peace*: This resembles the modern 'Wild horses wouldn't draw it out of me.' Fabian is saying, 'Keep quiet, though it is a torment to do so.'

63 *cars*: Chariots.

74 *scab*: Scurvy fellow.

81 *employment*: Business; matter.

83 *woodcock*: An easily trapped bird.
   gin: Snare.

84–5 *the spirit . . . to him*: May he take it into his head to read aloud.

84 *spirit of humours*: Genius who guides the capricious.

86–8 *These be her . . . great P's*: Not all these letters occur in the superscription, but they are given to Malvolio to make him sound bawdy. 'Cut' is the female genitals.

87–8 *makes . . . P's*: With a play on the meaning 'urinates'.

88 *in contempt of question*: Beyond all doubt.

91 *Soft*: Gently! (as he breaks the seal).

92 *impressure*: Stamp; seal.

Lucrece: Seal bearing the image of the Roman matron Lucretia, the model of chastity.

94 *liver and all*: Malvolio is deeply excited.

99–100 *The numbers altered*: The metre is changed!

102 *brock*: badger. Malvolio is burrowing for the letter's meaning.

106 *M.O.A.I. . . . my life*: Shakespeare scholars have been no quicker than Malvolio at solving this *fustian riddle*. An attractive suggestion is that the letters stand for I AM O (I am Olivia and this rules my conduct), but that Malvolio, sick of self-love, immediately applies them to himself, thus provoking Sir Toby's remark about a *cold scent*.

107 *fustian*: Wretched.

112 *staniel*: An inferior hawk.

checks at it: Swerves to pounce on it (a hawking term).

115 *formal capacity*: Normal intelligence.

115–16 *obstruction*: Difficulty.

117 *position*: Arrangement.

120–21 *Sowter will cry . . . rank as a fox*: Malvolio has missed the right meaning and is about to go full cry after his own interpretation, like a hound which has missed the hare's scent and picked up a fox's instead. *Sowter* means 'cobbler' and is presumably a name for an awkward hound.

125 *faults*: Breaks in the scent.

126 *consonancy*: Consistency.

127 *that suffers under probation*: That will stand up to investigation.

129 *O shall end*: 'O' could mean the hangman's noose. But if the riddle means 'I AM O', Fabian may be hoping that Malvolio will work it out.

135 *simulation*: Disguise.

135–6 *the former*: Referring to *I may command where I adore*.

139 *revolve*: Consider.

140 *born*: F has *become*. The sentence is repeated twice

later in the play, with *born* in each case, so we must
assume the compositor read 'borne' as 'become' –
a plausible error. Maria's letter is not italicized in F
after *revolve*, which suggests that only the beginning
of it was in the prompt book, and that this had to
be supplemented by the letter read out on the stage.
This is also suggested by the end of the letter, where
F reads *tht fortunate vnhappy   daylight and champian*
with an awkward space after *vnhappy*. The punctuation of the letter is also uncertain, by comparison
with the careful punctuation of the rest of the play.
A property letter would be less legible than the
prompt book, either because of rough handling or
because it was a piece of the author's manuscript,
and this might explain *become* as a misreading of
'borne'.

144 *slough*: A snake's old skin.

145 *opposite with*: Hostile towards.

146 *tang*: Resound.

146–7 *trick of singularity*: Affectation of oddness.

148 *yellow stockings*: Not only were these old-fashioned
by 1601, but they would be out of keeping with the
deep mourning of Olivia's household. It is hard to
believe that Olivia ever *commended* them, if she
abhorred the colour yellow (192). Probably the only
commendation is in this letter, and Shakespeare shows
us how Malvolio's imagination does the rest. On the
amorous connotations of yellow stockings, see
Introduction.

149 *cross-gartered*: Wearing garters which crossed at the
back of the knee and tied above it in front. This
custom was old-fashioned at the date of the play.

154 *Daylight . . . more*: Broad daylight and open country
couldn't make this more plain.

156 *baffle*: Disgrace (used of a knight).

157 *point-devise*: To the last detail.

158 *jade*: Deceive.

163 *habits*: Clothes.

164 *strange*: Aloof.

164 *stout*: Bold.

169 *dear*: Possibly F's *deero* is not a misprint for 'deere',
and we should read 'dear, O my sweet'.

173–4 *a pension . . . Sophy*: This is almost certainly an
allusion to the gifts, including 16,000 pistoles (gold
coins), heaped upon the English adventurer Sir
Anthony Shirley during his stay at the court of the
Shah (or *Sophy*) of Persia, Abbas the Great, in 1599.
Shakespeare could have read about the expedition in
a pamphlet called *The True Report of Sir Anthony
Shirley's Journey*, published in the autumn of 1600.

180 *gull-catcher*: One who traps fools.

183 *tray-trip*: A dicing game in which success depends
on throwing a three.

189 *aqua-vitae*: Spirits.

196 *a notable contempt*: An infamous disgrace.

198 *Tartar*: Tartarus (the classical name for hell).

III.1

0 *tabor*: Queen Elizabeth's jester Tarlton is shown in
a famous engraving playing a tabor, or small drum,
and a pipe. The only real break in the play's action
occurs between Acts II and III, and perhaps Feste
has been entertaining the audience in this interval
by playing his pipe and tabor.

1 *Save thee*: God save thee.

   live by: Make a living by.

8 *lies by*: Dwells near (playing on the meaning 'go to
bed with').

9 *stands by*: With a play on the meaning 'is upheld
by'.

12 *cheveril*: Kid leather.

14 *dally nicely*: Play subtly.

15 *wanton*: Equivocal. Feste goes on to play with the
meaning 'unchaste'.

19–20 *words . . . disgraced them*: This is often read as an
allusion to the Jesuit practice of equivocation. But
Feste can simply be moralizing by saying that frequent
demands for vows and pledges show that a man's
yea is no longer yea, nor his nay, nay.

22–4 *I can yield you . . . reason with them*: Feste, who is
a wise fool, here touches on one of the biggest problems in philosophy.

33 *pilchers*: Pilchards (shoaling fish, similar to herrings).

40 *your wisdom*: An ironic courtesy title.

41 *an*: If.
pass upon: Jest at.

43 *commodity*: Consignment.

45 *By my troth*: In faith.

48 *these*: Coins.

49 *use*: Interest.

50 *Pandarus*: The go-between in the medieval story of
Troilus and Cressida, on which Shakespeare wrote
a tragedy. Feste hints that he will further a meeting
between Olivia and Cesario if he is well tipped.

53–4 *begging but a beggar*: In allusion to the practice of
begging the guardianship of rich orphans from the
sovereign.

54 *Cressida was a beggar*: She became one in Henryson's
fifteenth-century poem, *The Testament of Cresseid*.

55 *conster*: Construe; explain.

56 *out of my welkin*: Not my affair.

56–7 *welkin . . . element*: In substituting a far-fetched word
like *welkin*, which means 'sky', for *element*,
Shakespeare may be defending Ben Jonson, whose
use of the word 'element' had been satirized in a
play by Thomas Dekker, *Satiromastix* (1601).

58–9 *This fellow is wise . . . kind of wit*: This idea about
the professional fool is a commonplace of the time,
but it is possible that Shakespeare is remembering a set
of verses in Robert Armin's *Quips upon Question* (1600):

> A merry man is often thought unwise;
> Yet mirth in modesty's loved of the wise.
> Then say, should he for a fool go,
> When he's a more fool that accounts him so?
> Many men descant on another's wit
> When they have less themselves in doing it.

62 *like the haggard, check at every feather*: Swoop on every
small bird, as the wild hawk does. So Feste seizes
every opportunity for a jest.

65 *fit*: To the point.

66 *folly-fallen, quite taint their wit*: Stooping to folly,
considerably impair their reputation for common
sense.

69–70 *Dieu . . . serviteur*: God keep you, sir! And you too;
your servant!

72 *encounter*: Approach. Sir Toby speaks affectedly, but
Viola is a match for him.

73 *trade*: Business. Viola picks up the meaning 'a trading
voyage'.

75 *list*: Objective.

76 *Taste*: Try out.

80 *gate and entrance*: This phrase has a legal flavour,
and *gate* has a special legal meaning – 'the right to
pasture'. There is a pun on 'gait'.

81 *prevented*: Forestalled.

86 *pregnant*: Quick in understanding; receptive.
vouchsafed: Attentive.

88 *all ready*: Sir Andrew may write them down carefully.

95 *'Twas never merry world*: A catchphrase like the
modern 'Things have never been the same'.

96 *lowly feigning*: Pretended humility (in allusion to the
mistress–servant convention of courtly love).

107 *music from the spheres*: In ancient astronomy, still
widely accepted in Shakespeare's day, the universe
was thought of as being constructed of crystalline
spheres, so tightly fitted one inside the other that
they ground together as they turned and so produced
music.

110 *abuse*: Impose upon.

112 *hard construction*: Harsh interpretation.

115 *at the stake*: An image from bear-baiting.

117 *receiving*: Perception.

118 *cypress*: Piece of thin black gauze.

121 *grize*: Flight of steps (which is also the literal meaning

of *degree*, 120).

vulgar proof: Common experience.

124 *how apt the poor are to be proud*: Olivia refers to
herself rather than to Viola – 'Though you reject
me, I've something to be proud of – I have fallen
for a king among men.'

130 *proper*: Handsome.

131 *due west*: Olivia is telling Cesario to go and seek
his fortunes elsewhere.

westward ho: The cry of the Thames watermen
seeking passengers for the journey from the City or
Southwark to the court at Westminster.

132 *good disposition*: Equanimity (a natural happiness, as
distinct from that given by *Grace*).

136 *That you do think you are not what you are*: Viola
implies that Olivia is forgetting her worldly position.

137 *the same of you*: That you are not in fact what you
are in appearance. Olivia suspects Cesario is a high-
born youth in disguise.

145 *love's night is noon*: Love cannot be hid.

148 *I love thee so*: Olivia changes to the intimate second
person singular.

maugre: In spite of.

149 *wit*: Common sense.

150–53 *Do not extort . . . is better*: Do not force yourself
to think that because I have declared my love you
ought not to love me, but rather restrain this way
of thinking with the reflection that love which is freely
given is better than love that has been begged.

150 *clause*: Premise.

151 *For that*: Because.

III.2

10 *argument*: Proof.

12 *'Slight*: By God's light!

13–14 *oaths of judgement and reason*: Theologians laid down
three conditions for an oath: truth, judgement, reason.
Fabian omits truth.

15 *grand-jury men*: The task of a grand jury was to

decide if the evidence in particular cases was sufficient
to warrant a trial. Fabian goes on to produce evidence
that Olivia is in love with Sir Andrew.

18 *dormouse*: Sleeping (but with a further implied
meaning, 'timid').

23 *baulked*: Shirked.

23–4 *double gilt of this opportunity*: The most costly gold
plate was twice gilded. We still speak of a golden
opportunity.

25 *sailed into the north of my lady's opinion*: Earned my
lady's cold disdain.

26 *icicle on a Dutchman's beard*: This is probably an
allusion to William Barentz's Arctic voyage in 1596–7.

28 *policy*: Diplomacy.

30 *Brownist*: The Brownists were a religious group later
called 'Independents' and (in the nineteenth century)
'Congregationalists'. Their advocacy of a very demo-
cratic form of Church government seemed highly
seditious and 'political' to the average Elizabethan.
politician: Schemer.

31–2 *build me . . . Challenge me*: *me* here implies 'on my
advice'.

40 *curst*: Petulant.

42 *invention*: Inventiveness; matter.
with the licence of ink: With things you dare not say
to his face.

43 '*thou*'-*est*: Address him as 'thou' (that is, as an inferior).

45 *bed of Ware*: The famous Elizabethan bed, meas-
uring over ten feet each way, now in the Victoria
and Albert Museum in London.

46 *gall*: Sir Toby puns on the meanings 'an ingredient
of ink' and 'bitterness'.

47 *goose*: Symbolic of cowardice.

50 *cubiculo*: Bedroom (Italian – another affected term
from Sir Toby).

51 *manikin*: Puppet.

57 *wain-ropes*: Waggon-ropes pulled by oxen.

58 *hale*: Drag.

60 *anatomy*: Cadaver.

63 *youngest wren of nine*: A wren lays nine or ten eggs and the last bird hatched is usually the smallest. This justifies the emendation from F's *youngest Wren of mine*, which has little meaning.

64 *the spleen*: A fit of laughter.

68 *impossible passages of grossness*: Wildly improbable statements (in Maria's letter).

71–2 *pedant that keeps a school i'the church*: Schoolmaster who, having no schoolhouse of his own, teaches in the church. The practice was old-fashioned by this period.

75–6 *the new map with the augmentation of the Indies*: Emmeric Mollineux's map of the world on a new projection, published in 1599 in Richard Hakluyt's *Principal Navigations*, has a mesh of rhumb lines, and is the first to show the whole of the East Indies, which are therefore an *augmentation*.

III.3

1 *troubled you*: To follow me to the city.

6 *not all*: Not only.

8 *jealousy*: Concern.

9 *skill-less in*: Unacquainted with.

12 *rather*: More speedily (the original meaning of the word).

16 *uncurrent*: Worthless (like coins out of currency).

17 *worth*: Means.
    conscience: Awareness of my debt to you.

19 *reliques*: Antiquities, sights.

24 *renown*: Make famous.

27 *the Count his galleys*: The Count's galleys.

29 *it would scarce be answered*: It would be difficult to make reparation.

30 *Belike*: Perhaps.

32–3 *Albeit the quality . . . argument*: Although at that time, and with the cause we had, bloodshed could have been justified.

35 *traffic's*: Trade's.

37 *lapsèd*: Apprehended.

40 *Elephant*: At the time this play was written, there was an inn called the Elephant in Southwark, near the Globe Theatre. The more famous Elephant and Castle, still in London's *south suburbs*, is not mentioned in documents until the middle of the seventeenth century.

41 *bespeak our diet*: Order our meals.

45 *Haply*: Perhaps.
   toy: Trifle.

47 *idle markets*: Unnecessary expenditure.

III.4

1 *He says he'll come*: Supposing he says he'll come.

2 *bestow of*: Give.

5 *sad and civil*: Grave and sedate.

9 *possessed*: By the devil.

22 *sonnet*: Song.
   Please one and please all: This is the refrain of a popular song of the time. Malvolio should perhaps squeak it out, to mark his transformation.

25–6 *Not black . . . my legs*: Not melancholy (melancholy being caused by the black bile) in spite of the melancholy colour of my stockings. There is a possible allusion to a ballad tune called 'Black and Yellow', and perhaps Malvolio hums a little of it.

26 *It*: Maria's letter.

27 *sweet Roman hand*: Fashionable new italic handwriting.

29–30 *Ay, sweetheart, and I'll come to thee*: This is a quotation from another popular song, of which the words are given in *Tarlton's Jests* (1601).

35 *daws*: Jackdaws. The remark has more point if Malvolio has been singing.

47–8 *thy yellow stockings*: In quoting the letter, Malvolio appears to be calling his mistress 'thou' and she echoes him in shocked surprise at this familiarity.

56 *midsummer madness*: A proverbial phrase; great heat was supposed to make dogs run mad.

58 *hardly*: Only with difficulty.

63 *miscarry*: Come to harm.

65 *come near me*: Begin to understand who I am.

71 *tang*: F has *langer*. The compositor had apparently no difficulty with the rather unusual word *tang* in II.5.146, which suggests that the letter and this passage were in different handwritings, and that here the word ended with a flourish.

74 *the habit of some sir of note*: The way of dressing of some very important personage (perhaps Sir William Knollys).

75 *limed*: Snared.

76 *fellow*: This word originally meant 'companion', but was used to inferiors, with polite condescension, from the fourteenth century onwards. Malvolio flatters himself Olivia uses it of him as an equal.

79 *scruple*: Malvolio plays on the meanings 'doubt' and 'minute quantity'.

80 *incredulous*: Incredible.

84 *in the name of sanctity*: Sir Toby invokes holy powers before his encounter with the possessed Malvolio.

85 *drawn in little*: Contracted to minute size (like Milton's devils in Pandaemonium).

Legion: Used of the many devils possessing the madman described in Mark 5:9.

89–90 *private*: Privacy.

96 *Let me alone*: Let me deal with this.

102 *wisewoman*: Herbalist.

109 *move*: Upset.

111 *rough*: Violent.

112 *bawcock*: Fine bird.

113 *chuck*: Chicken.

115 *biddy*: Chickabiddy. Sir Toby is clucking encouragingly at Malvolio.

116 *gravity*: A sober, mature man.

cherry-pit: Children's game played with cherry-stones.

117 *collier*: Coal-vendor (in allusion to the devil's blackness).

123 *element*: Sphere of existence.

126 *played upon a stage*: This kind of theatrical bravado is found also in *Julius Caesar*, III.1.111–16, and *Antony and Cleopatra*, V.2.216–21. It does not imply that

Twelfth Night was not originally acted on a stage.

128 *genius*: Soul.

130–31 *take air, and taint*: Be exposed, and so spoilt. The Elizabethans thought fresh air bad for many fevers.

133 *quieter*: Freer from Malvolio's interference.

134–5 *dark room and bound*: This was the usual treatment for insanity in the period. 'Love' (says Rosalind) 'is merely a madness and, I tell you, deserves as well a dark house and a whip as madmen do' (*As You Like It*, III.2.383–4).

139 *to the bar*: This is unexplained. It may mean the bar dividing the benchers from the students in hall in the Inns of Court.

139–40 *a finder of madmen*: One of a jury appointed to find out if an accused person was insane.

141 *matter for a May morning*: Sport fit for a holiday.

144 *saucy*: With a pun on the meanings 'impudent' and 'piquant'.

149 *admire*: Marvel.

151–2 *keeps you from the blow of the law*: Shelters you from the law (that is, from being accused of causing a breach of the peace).

154 *thou liest in thy throat*: If Sir Andrew's letter is not as senseless as Fabian thinks, Sir Andrew is postulating a statement by Cesario: 'You are angry because of the Lady Olivia's attentions to me', in order to have grounds for calling him a liar.

161–2 *thou kill'st me like a rogue and a villain*: Sir Andrew's effort to avoid any actionable abuse, or any threat of violence towards his opponent, would have delighted an audience of law students.

163 *o' the windy side*: On the safe side (because you can't be scented out).

166–7 *my hope*: Of winning – but Sir Andrew is made to appear as if he is in hope of something better than salvation.

167–8 *as thou usest him*: As thy usage of him deserves (not at all, in fact).

171 *commerce*: Conference.

173 *Scout me for him*: I want you to keep a look-out for
     him.

174 *bum-baily*: Bailiff, or sheriff's officer, who shadowed
     a debtor in order to arrest him.

178 *approbation*: Credit.
     proof: Trial; testing.

186 *clodpole*: Blockhead.

192 *cockatrices*: Mythical monsters able to kill with a
     glance.

193 *Give them way*: Keep out of their way.

194 *presently*: Immediately.

195 *horrid*: Terrifying.

198 *unchary*: Unguardedly.
     on't: On a *heart of stone*, in allusion to the Elizabethan
     custom of making payment of a debt on a known
     stone in a church.

202 *With the same 'haviour*: In the same manner.

204 *jewel*: Jewel-set miniature.

208 *That honour . . . give*: That honour may grant, when
     requested, without compromising itself.

212–13 *Well, come again tomorrow. Fare thee well . . . bear
        my soul to hell*: The conclusive-sounding couplet
        here, and the fact that the action from this point to
        the end of the act can be thought of as taking place
        in the street outside Olivia's garden, would justify
        a modern director's treating the remainder of this
        act as a separate scene. On the Elizabethan stage,
        however, the action is continuous. Sir Toby and
        Fabian come forward and intercept Viola outside the
        door (or the curtain concealing the back of the stage)
        by which Olivia has just left. Then Sir Toby crosses
        the stage and either goes out by the farthest door
        to bring Sir Andrew back at *Why, man, he's a very
        devil* (267), or, finding him in view of the audience,
        engages him in conversation and brings him down-
        stage so that *Why, man* are the first words heard
        by the audience. Sir Toby and Fabian then coax the
        duellists into coming face to face, and as soon as
        they do so Antonio makes his dramatic entry.

218 *despite*: Defiance.

219–20 *Dismount thy tuck*: Draw thy sword.

220 *yare*: Prompt.

223 *remembrance*: Recollection.

227 *opposite*: Opponent.

228 *withal*: With.

230 *unhatched*: This means either 'not marked in battle' or 'never drawn'.

231 *on carpet consideration*: For non-military services to the Crown (usually financial ones at that period).

235 *Hob, nob*: Come what may (literally, have it or have it not).

239 *taste*: Test.
    quirk: Peculiarity.

241 *computent*: To be reckoned with.

245 *meddle*: Engage in combat.

248 *know of*: Inquire from.

250 *purpose*: Intention.

255 *mortal arbitrement*: Decision of the matter by mortal combat.

259 *form*: Appearance.

265 *Sir Priest*: *Sir* here stands for '*Dominus*', the title given to a graduate and thence used of a clergyman.

268 *firago*: Virago. The word means a fighting woman, but was used of both sexes in Shakespeare's day.

269 *stuck-in*: Thrust (from the Italian fencing term, '*stoccata*').

269–70 *mortal motion*: Deadly movement.

270 *it is inevitable*: It cannot be averted.

270–71 *on the answer, he pays you*: He counters your return blow.

272 *to the Sophy*: See note to II.5.173–4. Shakespeare may have learned from his former colleague Will Kemp, who had met Sir Anthony Shirley on his return from Persia, that Sir Anthony's brother, Sir Robert, had stayed on in Persia to reorganize the Shah's army.

276 *An*: If.

280 *make the motion*: Put the proposal.

281 *perdition of souls*: Killing.

282 *Marry*: An asseveration – originally 'By Mary'.

286 *He is as horribly conceited*: He has as terrifying an idea.

298 *duello*: Code of duelling.

309 *an undertaker*: One who undertakes another's quarrel.

314 *that I promised*: The horse.

320 *favour*: Face.

324 *answer*: Make reparation for.

325–6 *What will you do . . . purse*: Antonio's appeal, even in a desperate situation, expresses his concern for Sebastian.

328 *amazed*: Bewildered; dazed.

329 *be of comfort*: Do not grieve.

335 *having*: Resources.

336 *my present*: What I have at present.

337 *coffer*: Money (literally, chest).

339–40 *Is't possible . . . persuasion*: Is it possible that the claims of my past kindnesses can fail to move you?

346 *vainness*: Boasting.

352 *sanctity of love*: Love as for a sacred object.

354 *venerable*: Worthy to be venerated.

356 *vild*: Vile (a common Elizabethan form of the word, kept here for euphony).

358–9 *In nature . . . the unkind*: Although there may seem to be deformities in nature, the only real deformity is a hard heart.

361 *o'er-flourished*: Richly decorated. Elaborately carved or painted chests were a feature of prosperous Elizabethan homes.

365 *so do not I*: Why do I not believe myself (my hope that my brother is alive)?

368 *Come hither*: Sir Toby and his friends draw contemptuously aside, leaving Viola to speak her thoughts in couplets, the common form for adages, or *sage saws*.

369 *sage saws*: Wise sayings; aphorisms.

370–71 *I my brother know . . . glass*: I know my brother is the image of me. On the possibility that Shakespeare was here remembering his dead son Hamnet, survived by his twin sister, Judith, see Introduction.

374 *prove*: Prove to be so.

376 *dishonest*: Dishonourable.

380 *religious in it*: Behaving as if it were a principle of his faith (to be cowardly).

381 *'Slid*: A mild oath – originally, 'God's eyelid'.

385 *event*: Result.

386 *yet*: After all.

IV.1

5 *held out*: Kept up.

9 *vent*: Void; get rid of.

13 *lubber*: Overgrown boy.

14 *cockney*: Pampered child. Feste is saying 'How affected everyone is getting, using words like "vent"!' *ungird thy strangeness*: Stop being stand-offish.

15 *vent*: Utter; say. This meaning, developed from the meaning 'get rid of' (see 9 above) was to become common in the seventeenth century.

17 *foolish Greek*: Buffoon. The expression is usually found in the form 'merry Greek'.

22 *after fourteen years' purchase*: The usual Elizabethan price of land was the equivalent of twelve years' rent, so *fourteen years' purchase* was a lot of money, and the phrase means 'at a price'.

33 *action of battery*: As Sir Andrew struck the first blow he has, of course, no case: another joke for the law students.

38 *put up your iron*: Sheathe your sword (said ironically; Sebastian has only used the hilt of his dagger). *fleshed*: Initiated into fighting; blooded.

43 *malapert*: Impudent.

50 *Rudesby*: Boor.

52 *uncivil*: Barbarous. *extent*: Assault (originally a legal term).

55 *botched up*: Crudely contrived.

57 *deny*: Refuse. *Beshrew*: Curse.

58 *started*: Roused (a hunting term). *heart*: With a pun on 'hart' and a use of the familiar conceit that lovers exchange hearts.

59 *What relish is in this*: What am I to make of this?
   relish: Taste.
60 *Or*: Either.
61 *Lethe*: The mythical river of forgetfulness.
63 *Would thou'dst*: If only you would.

IV.2

 2 *Sir*: A title used for a clergyman; see note to III.4.265.
   Topas: All precious and semi-precious stones were
   supposed to have healing properties; the topaz cured
   lunacy.
   curate: Parish priest.
 8 *said*: Called.
   an honest man and a good housekeeper: A good sort,
   and hospitable.
 9 *careful*: Serious-minded.
10 *competitors*: Confederates.
12 *Bonos dies*: Good day (mock Latin).
12–13 *old hermit of Prague*: An authority invented in parody
   of pedantic name-dropping.
14 *Gorboduc*: Legendary early British king, hero of a
   famous sixteenth-century play.
   that that is, is: Feste takes off the axioms of medieval
   philosophy which often sound absurdly self-evident
   to the layman.
20 *within*: In F, the stage direction *Maluolio within*
   precedes the speech-prefix *Mal.*, as a warning to the
   actor to be ready. See An Account of the Text.
25 *hyperbolical*: Boisterous. Feste is addressing the devil
   which has possessed Malvolio.
33–4 *that house is dark*: A dark house was the term for a
   darkened room in which a madman was confined.
   The expression occurs in the fifth story of Rich's
   Farewell to Military Profession.
36 *bay windows*: These were the rage of the period,
   when great houses were laughed at for being 'more
   glass than wall'.
36–7 *barricadoes*: Barricades. These and *ebony* wood are
   the most opaque things Feste can think of. His joke
   is of the 'clear as mud' type.

37 *clerestories*: A range of windows high up in a wall.

42 *darkness*: A three-day darkness was one of the plagues of Egypt described in Exodus 10.

47 *abused*: Ill treated.

48 *constant question*: Question and answer on a normal topic.

49 *Pythagoras*: A Greek philosopher who held the theory of the transmigration of souls; the same soul could inhabit in succession the bodies of different kinds of creatures – fish, birds and animals, as well as men.

51 *haply*: Perhaps.

62 *I am for all waters*: I can turn my hand to anything (with a pun on 'water' in the sense of the brilliance or lustre of a precious or semi-precious stone such as a topaz).

69–70 *the upshot*: To its final outcome (an archery term, meaning 'the decisive shot').

71 *Hey Robin, jolly Robin*: An early Tudor setting to this poem is given in The Songs. The words have been attributed to Sir Thomas Wyatt.

74 *perdy*: French *par Dieu*; an adjuration.

86 *besides your five wits*: Out of your mind (the five wits being the five faculties of the mind: common wit, imagination, fantasy, estimation and memory).

91 *propertied me*: Treated me as a mere property.

93 *face*: Brazen.

94 *Advise you*: Be careful.

97 *bibble-babble*: There may be some echo here of a controversy which raged round the preacher John Darrell, who claimed to have successfully cured several people possessed by devils. In 1600 Darrell published *A True Narration*, in which the victims are said on three occasions to have called the Scriptures 'bible-bable'. But the expression was quite a common one.

100 *God buy you*: God be with you.

101–2 *Marry . . . I will*: With a pun on *Marry* used as a mild oath and as meaning 'wed'.

104 *shent*: Scolded.

109 *Well-a-day*: Alas!

121–8 *I am gone, sir . . . goodman devil*: This may have
been recited and not sung.

123 *old Vice*: A character who defied the devil in the
early Tudor interludes which developed from
the morality plays. He was one ancestor of the
Elizabethan stage fool.

127 *Pare thy nails*: A passage in *Henry V* – 'this roaring
devil i'th'old play, that everyone may pare his nails
with a wooden dagger' (IV.4.69–70) – suggests that
this was a familiar piece of stage business.

IV.3

6 *there he was*: He had been there.
credit: Report.

11 *accident*: Unexpected happening.

12 *instance*: Example.
discourse: Reasoning.

17 *sway*: Rule.

18 *Take and give . . . dispatch*: Olivia receives reports
from her household and gives them orders in return.

21 *deceivable*: Deceptive.

24 *chantry by*: Nearby chapel (a chantry being an
endowed chapel where masses were said for the soul
of the founder).

26 *Plight me the full assurance*: A ceremony of betrothal,
in the presence of a priest, was as binding a contract
as the actual marriage service.

29 *Whiles*: Until.

31 *birth*: Nobility.

V.I

5–6 *This is to give a dog . . . dog again*: John Manningham's
diary, which records the first known performance of
Twelfth Night, also gives us the source of this saying:
'Mr Francis Curle told me how one Doctor Bulleyn,
the Queen's kinsman, had a dog which he doted on,
so much that the Queen, understanding of it,
requested he would grant her one desire, and he
should have whatsoever he would ask. She demanded
his dog. He gave it, and – "Now, Madam," quoth

he, "you promised to give me my desire." "I will,"
quoth she. "Then I pray you, give me my dog again.'"

8 *trappings*: Bits and pieces. Feste, who belongs to no
one, is irritated by Orsino's tone.

19–21 *conclusions . . . armatives*: Similar jests of the period
are based on the assumption that a girl's 'No, no,
no, no!' could be interpreted as 'Yes, yes!'

27 *double-dealing*: Punning on the meanings 'a double
donation' and 'duplicity'.

30 *your grace*: There is a pun here on (1) the form of
address to a duke, and (2) Orsino's share of divine
grace which should prevent his listening to *ill
counsel*.

34 *Primo, secundo, tertio*: One, two, three (Latin for
first, second, third – probably the beginning of a
children's counting game).

35 *the third pays for all*: The words *at this throw* in
Orsino's next speech, meaning 'at this throw of the
dice', suggest that Feste is here quoting the gambler's
proverb which is best known in the form 'third time
lucky'.

36 *Saint Bennet*: St Benedict. Shakespeare may have
been thinking of the London church just across the
river from the Globe.

42 *lullaby to your bounty*: May your generosity sleep
well (continuing the metaphor used by Orsino).

46 *anon*: Soon.

50 *Vulcan*: The smith of the gods in Roman mythology.

51 *baubling*: Paltry.

52 *unprizable*: Worthless.

53 *scatheful*: Destructive.

54 *bottom*: Ship.

55 *loss*: The losers.

58 *fraught*: Cargo.
   Candy: Candia (now Crete).

61 *desperate of shame and state*: Recklessly disregarding
both the harm a quarrel would do to his character
and the danger in which it would place him.

62 *brabble*: Brawl.

64 *put strange speech upon me*: Spoke to me in a strange manner.

65 *distraction*: Madness.

68 *dear*: Dire.

77 *wrack*: Shipwrecked person.

79 *retention*: Power of holding back.

81 *pure*: Purely; only.

86 *face me out of*: Deny to my face.

87 *removèd thing*: Estranged being.

97 *Three months*: Actually Viola has been only three days in Orsino's service when she is sent to Olivia, and after that the action is very rapid. But the inconsistency passes unnoticed in the theatre. See Introduction.

104 *Good, my lord*: A polite request to Orsino to let Viola speak first.

107 *fat and fulsome*: Nauseating.

111 *ingrate*: Ungrateful.

114 *become him*: Be fitting for him.

116 *th'Egyptian thief*: This alludes to a story told by Heliodorus in his *Ethiopica*, which was popular in a translation in Shakespeare's day. The thief was Thyamis, a brigand who attempted to kill his captive Chariclea to prevent her falling into the hands of his own captors.

119 *non-regardance*: Contempt.

121 *screws*: Wrenches.

124 *tender*: Hold; esteem.

126 *in his master's spite*: To the mortification of his master.

134 *More by all mores*: More beyond all comparisons.

137 *detested*: Denounced with an oath; execrated.

143 *sirrah*: A contemptuous mode of address.

145 *strangle thy propriety*: Suppress your identity as my husband (perhaps with a play on a further meaning of *propriety*, 'ownership' — 'the fact that I am yours').

163 *a grizzle*: Grey hairs.
    case: Skin.

165 *trip*: This can mean 'headlong speed' or 'trap', and

probably means both here; Orsino calls Cesario both a deceiver and a fast worker.

169 *little*: A little.

171 *presently*: At once.

174 *coxcomb*: Pate.

178–9 *incardinate*: Sir Andrew's error for 'incarnate'.

181 *'Od's lifelings*: God's life!

188 *set nothing by*: Think nothing of.

189 *halting*: Limping.

191 *othergates*: Otherwise.

196 *set*: Closed.

197 *passy-measures pavin*: This was a stately dance to a strain consisting of at least eight semibreves, and Sir Toby, an expert on the dance, is perhaps reminded of it by mention of *eight i'the morning*. He means that Dick Surgeon's slowness in answering his call passes all measure. The phrase must have been a little puzzling to the copyist or compositor, because *pavin* appears as *panyn* in F. A more common form of the word is 'pavane'.

201–2 *be dressed*: Have our wounds dressed.

203 *coxcomb*: Blockhead.

204 *gull*: Fool.

207 *the brother of my blood*: My own brother.

208 *with wit and safety*: Having any sense at all of my own safety.

213 *habit*: Garb.

214 *perspective*: Optical device. This could not have been a stereoscopic device, as these were not invented until the early eighteenth century. Besides, a stereoscopic device makes two images into one, and what Shakespeare has in mind here is something that makes one image into two. It could be a trick painting on a surface folded concertina-wise, so that it appeared to be two different paintings when viewed from two different angles. Or it could be a theatrical illusion of the Pepper's Ghost type in which, by the use of mirrors, one figure was turned into two. Such illusions were known and practised on the Continent

early in the seventeenth century.

218 *Fear'st*: Do you doubt.

224 *that deity in my nature*: Ubiquity; only God can be
in two places at once.

231 *suited*: Dressed.

232–3 *If spirits . . . fright us*: One Elizabethan theory about
ghosts was that they were evil spirits assuming the
appearance of dead people.

234 *dimension*: Bodily form.
grossly: Substantially.

235 *participate*: Have in common with others.

236 *as the rest goes even*: As everything fits in with your
being my sister.

243 *record*: Recollection.

246 *lets*: Hinders.

249 *cohere*: Accord together.
jump: Agree.

252 *weeds*: Clothes.

257 *to her bias drew*: Obeyed her inclination (a metaphor
from the game of bowls).

260 *maid and man*: Virgin youth.

262 *as yet the glass seems true*: As in fact the 'perspective' turns out not to be an illusion after all.

263 *wrack*: Shipwreck.

268 *that orbèd continent*: The sphere of the sun.

272 *action*: Legal charge.

273 *durance*: Imprisonment.

275 *enlarge*: Free.

277 *distract*: Disturbed in his mind.

278 *extracting*: That drew everything else out of my
thoughts. Olivia is playing a variation upon *distract*
in the previous line.

281–2 *Beelzebub at the stave's end*: The devil at bay.

284 *epistles*: Feste puns on the general sense 'letters' and
the special sense 'New Testament letters'. There is
a reference to the sixteenth-century liturgical controversies about when the gospel for the day should
be read, or *delivered*.
skills not: Doesn't matter.

287–8 *delivers*: Speaks the words of.

293 *vox*: The right voice. This was a technical term of Elizabethan public speaking.

294 *Prithee*: I pray thee (equivalent to 'please').

296 *perpend*: Be attentive.

316 *proper*: Own.

317 *apt*: Ready.

318 *quits you*: Releases you from service.

330 *from it*: Differently.

331 *invention*: Composition.

333 *in the modesty of honour*: With a modest regard for your reputation.

334 *lights*: Signals; indications.

337 *lighter*: Lesser.

341 *geck and gull*: Butt and dupe.

344 *character*: Hand.

348 *presupposed*: Previously enjoined.

350 *This practice . . . thee*: This trick has been very cunningly played on you.

359–60 *Upon some stubborn . . . him*: In consequence of his stiff-necked and unfriendly behaviour to which we took exception.

361 *importance*: Importunity.

367 *poor fool*: Said affectionately.
    baffled: Treated shamefully.

374 *whirligig*: Spinning top.

375 *pack*: A word used of a group of plotters.

379 *convents*: Calls us together.

386 *When that I was and a little tiny boy*: The confusion of the fourth stanza suggests that this was a folk song. Another stanza of it is said or sung by the Fool in *King Lear*. Modern actors of Feste like to sing it with pathos, but probably it was intended as a 'jig' or cheerful conclusion to a comedy. See The Songs for the tune to which it is often sung in the theatre.

388 *toy*: Trifle.

400 *tosspots*: Sots.

PENGUIN SHAKESPEARE

ANTONY AND CLEOPATRA
WILLIAM SHAKESPEARE

A battle-hardened soldier, Antony is one of the three leaders of the
Roman world. But he is also a man in the grip of an all-consuming
passion for the exotic and tempestuous Queen of Egypt. And when
their life of pleasure together is threatened by the encroaching politics
of Rome, the conflict between love and duty has devastating
consequences.

This book includes a general introduction to Shakespeare's life and the
Elizabethan theatre, a separate introduction to *Antony and Cleopatra*,
a chronology of his works, suggestions for further reading, an essay
discussing performance options on both stage and screen, and a
commentary.

Edited by Emrys Jones

With an introduction by René Weis

General Editor: Stanley Wells

Penguin Shakespeare

KING JOHN
WILLIAM SHAKESPEARE

Under the rule of King John, England is forced into war when the
French challenge the legitimacy of John's claim to the throne and
determine to install his nephew Arthur in his place. But political
principles, hypocritically flaunted, are soon forgotten, as the French
and English kings form an alliance based on cynical self-interest. And
as the desire to cling to power dominates England's paranoid and
weak-willed king, his country is threatened with disaster.

This book includes a general introduction to Shakespeare's life and the
Elizabethan theatre, a separate introduction to *King John*, a chronology
of his works, suggestions for further reading, an essay discussing
performance options on both stage and screen, and a commentary.

Edited by R. L. Smallwood

With an introduction by Eugene Giddens

General Editor: Stanley Wells

PENGUIN SHAKESPEARE

MACBETH
WILLIAM SHAKESPEARE

Promised a golden future as ruler of Scotland by three sinister witches, Macbeth murders the king to ensure his ambitions come true. But he soon learns the meaning of terror – killing once, he must kill again and again, and the dead return to haunt him. A story of war, witchcraft and bloodshed, *Macbeth* also depicts the relationship between husbands and wives, and the risks they are prepared to take to achieve their desires.

This book includes a general introduction to Shakespeare's life and the Elizabethan theatre, a separate introduction to *Macbeth*, a chronology of his works, suggestions for further reading, an essay discussing performance options on both stage and screen, and a commentary.

Edited by George Hunter

With an introduction by Carol Rutter

General Editor: Stanley Wells

PENGUIN SHAKESPEARE

THE MERCHANT OF VENICE
WILLIAM SHAKESPEARE

A noble but impoverished Venetian asks a friend, Antonio, for a loan to impress an heiress. His friend agrees, but is forced to borrow the sum from a cynical Jewish moneylender, Shylock, and signs a chilling contract to honour the debt with a pound of his own flesh. A complex and controversial comedy, *The Merchant of Venice* explores prejudice and the true nature of justice.

This book includes a general introduction to Shakespeare's life and the Elizabethan theatre, a separate introduction to *The Merchant of Venice*, a chronology of his works, suggestions for further reading, an essay discussing performance options on both stage and screen, and a commentary.

Edited by W. Moelwyn Merchant

With an introduction by Peter Holland

General Editor: Stanley Wells

PENGUIN SHAKESPEARE

TIMON OF ATHENS
WILLIAM SHAKESPEARE

After squandering his wealth with prodigal generosity, a rich Athenian gentleman finds himself deep in debt. Unshaken by the prospect of bankruptcy, he is certain that the friends he has helped so often will come to his aid. But when they learn his wealth is gone, he quickly finds that their promises fall away to nothing in this tragic exploration of power, greed, and loyalty betrayed.

This book includes a general introduction to Shakespeare's life and the Elizabethan theatre, a separate introduction to *Timon of Athens*, a chronology of his works, suggestions for further reading, an essay discussing performance options on both stage and screen, and a commentary.

Edited by G. R. Hibbard

With an introduction by Nicholas Walton

General Editor: Stanley Wells

PENGUIN SHAKESPEARE

MUCH ADO ABOUT NOTHING
WILLIAM SHAKESPEARE

A vivacious woman and a high-spirited man both claim that they are determined never to marry. But when their friends trick them into believing that each harbours secret feelings for the other, they begin to question whether their witty banter and sharp-tongued repartee conceals something deeper. Schemes abound, misunderstandings proliferate and matches are eventually made in this sparkling and irresistible comedy.

This book includes a general introduction to Shakespeare's life and the Elizabethan theatre, a separate introduction to *Much Ado About Nothing*, a chronology of his works, suggestions for further reading, an essay discussing performance options on both stage and screen, and a commentary.

Edited by R. A. Foakes

With an introduction by Janette Dillon

General Editor: Stanley Wells

PENGUIN SHAKESPEARE